# CAMPSIGHT

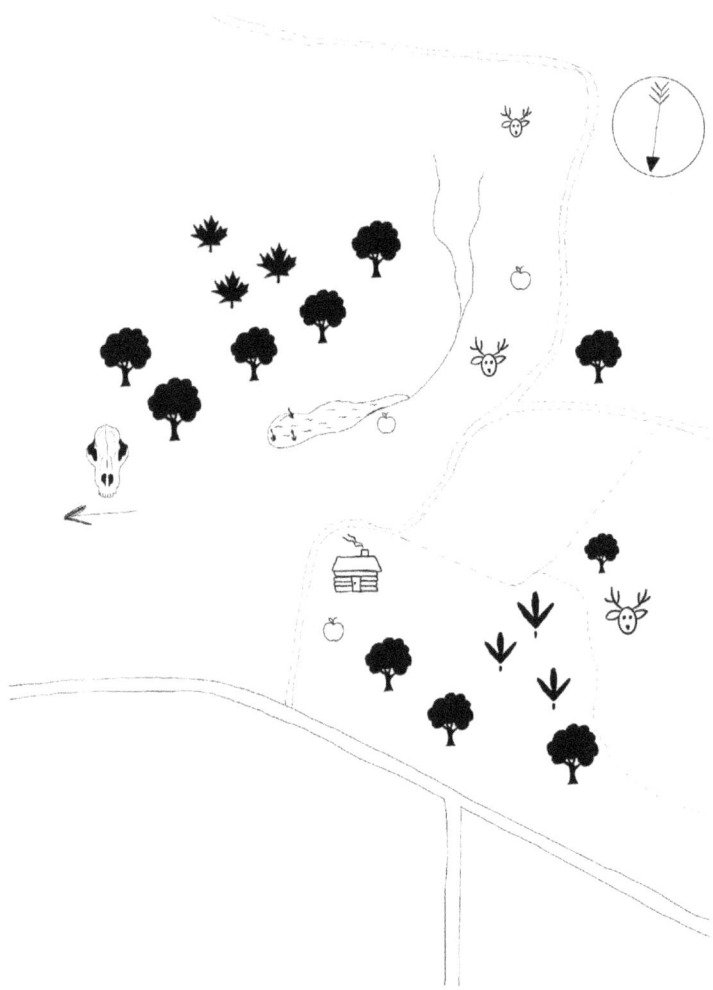

# CAMPSIGHT

## THE (MOSTLY) GOOD THINGS ABOUT A
## LIFE SPENT OUTDOORS

Iain Eastman

Published by East Branch Book Ranch
www.eastbranchbooks.com

*While the people, conversations, and events in this book are presented as accurately as I can recall, it is entirely likely that I have screwed up some significant detail regarding time, space, or human intelligence that I'm sure to hear about later. Many apologies.*

*For Lou and Sheila, who showed me how to do everything.*
*For MB, who believed that I could.*

# Contents

"The Pope's Homers would soon get properly distributed."
                                                                                  - Henry David Thoreau

Every book that features a cabin, has the main character spend time in a cabin, mentions living in the woods, mentions the word cabin at all, even in reference to an airplane, has to start with a quote from *Walden*. It's practically a literary law, or so I'm led to believe. Authors usually pick the same passage about going to the woods in order to "live deliberately." This quote is way better, it just doesn't work as well when divorced from the rest of the book. Now that that's out of the way, I promise to only bring up Thoreau once more in the following pages. There are plenty of books about cabin living and the yearning for simpler times and getting in touch with nature and self and so on. And really, you should probably go read one of those instead, something like *A Year in the Maine Woods*, or *A Sand County Almanac*. Then, if you're like me and still desperate to escape, even if only vicariously, even if only for a short while, then this book may be of some use to you.

# Introduction

The day began much the same as all the others lately, a race between my dogs and my bladder as to which would get me up first. For some reason I always think I can stave off the inevitable – if I just tap my foot enough, clench the right muscles just so, then maybe I'll fall back asleep. It's never worked. I'm not one to give up, however, so every morning plays out the same as the one before. I throw off the top half of the flannel lined sleeping bag and reluctantly, yet hastily, get dressed. The dogs, as usual, are a heartbeat behind the necessities of biology, or perhaps they are just more patient. They bark excitedly as we head down the stairs. I don't bother to stop at the bathroom. If the outdoors is good enough for them, it's good enough for me. Better, in fact. "Unzip your fly, piss hearty" as Abbey said. We take our time, the dogs and I, adding to the dew that has settled on the milkweed and goldenrod, the dandelion and white clover. There's a space of time now, only a couple of minutes, where there are no regrets, no past, no obligations and no future. There's only now. Those couple minutes are among the best stretches of time in my day, month, year - sweet air and sweet relief. Welcome to another morning.

A minor disruption to the morning reverie – the dogs need fed and I need coffee. If I was smart enough to set up the coffee maker the night before, it would take but the push of a button. I am not smart enough to set up the coffee maker the night before, so I instead fumble to find the correct light switch – it's barely sunup yet – and assemble the jigsaw puzzle that is caffeination. I was once accused of being a Luddite. After I looked it up to decide whether or not I should be offended, I proudly declared myself one. I was stupid and in my twenties then. I've since come around on the idea of technology – the microwave, GPS, Spotify. The programmable coffee maker.

Mug in hand, I return to the back porch. The dew was heavy last night and there is nowhere dry to sit. The dew is heavy every night here. I place the minimum amount of ass on the edge of the porch, planting my bare feet in the cold, wet grass, and set down my mug. Steam curls and wafts away, disappearing with the morning dew. The dogs turn impatient circles at my feet, eager to know the day's agenda. I can't relax and simply enjoy this moment for what it is, because I, too, am eager to know the day's agenda.

I suffer from an inability to enjoy things as they are. I may daydream about wilderness and solitude, but the moment I am granted either I begin to pine for civilization and company. Civilization in the form of internet and restaurants, company in the form of my wife. She doesn't make it up here often, to the cabin. And if she did, I would probably fantasize about being up here alone. Alone is rare, though, as I often have two of my three children with me (when I wasn't looking, the oldest one, a high schooler, went and got himself a life and a job), and my father is often a fixture here as well. But right now they're all still in bed, and it's just me and the dogs and the sunrise.

This land has been in my family for more generations than I know. Somewhere there is a record of the first Eastman to purchase or be granted this parcel. I've even held the compiled history in my hands, though I didn't understand the significance of it at the time. I am not troubled, because I know that the history is preserved and accessible should I ever require it. My earliest memory tied to this place is of a massive walnut tree standing next to a shingled pavilion. There's a swing of some sort (rope, tire?) in there somewhere. I also remember blackberries, and the novel discovery that you could get food from somewhere other than the refrigerator or grocery store. The camp, as it's known, marked my introduction to the idea of "living off the land." We had a sizeable garden in our backyard growing up, but something about letting nature do the work for you was . . . different. There was no tilling or fertilizing for these blackberries, they were just there. There and available and tasty. And the surrounding acreage was full of promises of similar discoveries.

I doubt I visited that property more than once or twice a year as a kid. The distance, my parents' work schedules, the lack of someplace to go to the bathroom. Yet still it loomed large in my mind. Sometime in middle school my oldest sister gave me a copy of Jean Craighead George's *My Side of the Mountain*, and the value of that land skyrocketed in my mind. I envisioned camping out in a hollowed-out tree and living off the land like a true mountain man. Maybe I'd find an injured bird or a fawn that I could nurse back to health and keep as a pet. I'd hunt and fish and forage and learn to tie all sorts of complicated knots in rope that I had braided myself from fibers collected in the vicinity. I would need nobody and nobody would need me. There was limitless potential.

Jobs, pickup trucks, girls, school – as I got older all manner of things took me away from that land. I never lost interest, but the pecking order of priority is fickle when you're sixteen. By the time I moved out of state for college, hunting and fishing and the camp in general had become background noise. I made a couple trips out there with my college roommate, a handy excuse to take a road-trip and drink ourselves stupid. By that time the old dugout dirt roof camp house had collapsed and a two-piece prefab trailer had been hauled up to replace it. My roommate and I made the brilliant decision to pay a visit in the winter of '98. It got cold enough overnight that our boots froze into non-malleable contortions of leather and the whiskey bottles provided their own ice. We didn't care, we were there to drink, shoot stuff, and pretend like we were roughing it.

After graduation I took a job out of state in the other direction, moving to Baltimore in the summer of 2000. I was now a five- or six-hour drive from the camp and, more importantly, I was completely swamped with working my first real person job as a high-school science teacher. Stress, angst, and alcoholism soon supplanted most everything else. I was single, overwhelmed, city-bound, and adrift. My morning commute pitted me against the rest of the rat race on four lanes of I-695, though it was usually before 6:00 AM when I left and traffic was lighter than it would be for the rest of the day. On weekends I would try to re-center myself by visiting the local state park, hiking under the I-95 overpass to get lost in what little wilderness the urban environment allowed. Time passed and life continued, a conveyor belt of predictability, unremarkable because of how scripted it all seemed. Marriage, house, children, rinse and repeat. I don't mean to come across as bitter or ungrateful, I did and still do love all those parts of my life, but I was a simply a placeholder, interchangeable with any of a hundred others doing the exact same thing.

So right here is where I had written a whole bunch of stuff about the mundanity of it all and futility and consumer driven zombie drone existence etc. etc. But that shit's depressing. The cure for this particular depression was moving back to the general vicinity of the family land in the summer of '08.

Proper cabin building became serious business around the summer of 2010, and things moved forward swiftly. There were no blueprints that I ever saw, just the thoughts in my father's head about how things should be constructed. I helped as much as possible for someone with a new job and a new baby, and visits to the property slowly became more frequent. Two hours, the length of time it now takes me to drive door to door, used to feel like an eternity. The only thing that can make the drive feel long now is when one of the dogs throws up in the backseat and you wonder how much longer you'll have to spend smelling hot, regurgitated dog food.

The cabin, more than anything, seemed to give me a reason to make the drive. First maybe only three or four times a year, then a dozen, and pretty soon I was spending more weekends there than not. Most of the stories in this book are about things that took place simply because that cabin exists. Even the ones that didn't take place there share a common sort of source material. Nature, the outdoors, wilderness and the things that belong to it – for me they hit like the first chord of an '80s hair metal power ballad. I once met someone who said he didn't trust people who didn't drink. I feel the same way about people who don't enjoy time spent in the company of nature. Edward Abbey had the desert southwest, John Muir had the Sierra Nevada, Aldo Leopold had Wisconsin. I have Warren County, Pennsylvania.

# Zebco

I can't remember the first time I went fishing. I'd guess that I was three or four years old. It was more than likely at a local lake that held lots of easy-to-catch bluegill. I probably fished with redworms, or perhaps mealworms, under a red and white bobber. Two things I can guarantee though; it was with my father, and I used a Zebco 800 series spincast reel with a star drag mounted to a five and a half foot Ugly Stik.

It was probably a combo deal, rod and reel for one low price at someplace like K-Mart. Six-pound test monofilament, pre-spooled, probably hadn't been changed in a few years. It was impressive the way that pole could bend almost double and then spring back without breaking. Nothing like my Grandfather's fly pole – look at that thing the wrong way and it might snap like uncooked spaghetti. The rod and reel lived in the basement of our house, along with some assorted tackle, a big case of Mr. Twister soft plastics in every color of the rainbow, some random camping gear, and a gun cleaning kit in a bright orange case. And a bunch of spiders.

I remember standing in my driveway, probably seven or eight years old at this point, practicing casting at a five-gallon bucket, a couple of washers tied to the end of the line to give it some weight. That rod and reel combo could cast a mile. Hit the release just right and it almost seemed to sing, line spooling out with a satisfying whir. You had to be careful because of the power lines that ran above the driveway, cast wrong and you'd get so wrapped up you'd have to cut the line, and who knows how much was left on the reel at this point? It might have been respooled in the intervening years, but if so I wasn't around to see it. I was more worried that I'd go all key-and-a-kite and get electrocuted through the line.

My dad bought a boat. It floated, the motor ran, and there was just enough level space to stand that you could cast off the bow. It had a folding seat perched atop a pole in the front, way too high to be stable or safe. Sitting in that seat I don't think my feet touched the deck, and whenever the boat made a turn I'd grab the sides of the seat with both hands, scared of falling into the lake. I vaguely remember a horse collar style lifejacket, so old and dry rotted it probably would have acted more like an anchor than a float. I preferred to sit on the thwart that was wrapped with outdoor carpet, my tennis shoes soaking up water on the aluminum bottom. Sitting in the bottom of the boat with me was the Ugly Stik with the Zebco reel. We'd motor to a small cove thick with lily pads, casting at old stumps trying to tease out the largemouths hiding there. I think the biggest fish I ever caught with that combo was a catfish out of that lake, couldn't have been more than a couple pounds, but I'd learned to thumb the drag and play the fish without breaking him off. I must have heard "Set the hook!" a hundred times before I knew what it actually meant, but the pole was forgiving and I landed more than I lost.

I graduated from hooks and bobbers to spinners and spoons, from bluegill and sunfish to browns and rainbows. Sunny summer afternoons on a lake were replaced with cold and snowy April mornings standing thigh deep in water so frigid your bones would stay cold for a week. I was still only eight or nine, but I was fishing with the men now. I don't know how my father ever got any fishing done, he probably didn't. I didn't know how to properly tie on a swivel, and even if I did, my fingers were too numb to obey the directions sent to them. I was really good at getting snagged. A lot. Usually on the far side of the stream (told you it would cast a mile.) I think I forced myself to learn to tie fishing knots because I felt bad for my father. But every year we went back. I can no longer remember the last time we fished that creek, though. At some point all the access went private, and I guess we found somewhere new to fish. I don't remember where that was either.

And then I quit fishing. Sometime around high school or college things got in the way and I just . . . didn't go anymore. After school I got a job in another state. Unfamiliar with the local waters, never having purchased anything fishing related for myself, hell, never having even bought my own fishing license – priorities change. I got married. Moved apartments. Bought a house. Had a kid. Had another. And then at one point, an opportunity to move back. My oldest was three at the time, just about old enough to start fishing. We made the jump. Back to Pennsylvania in the summer of '08, kid number three a couple years later. A couple dogs thrown in because I'm dumb that way.

And I started fishing again. Same old Ugly Stik, same old Zebco. My oldest son learned to fish using that same setup, my second son as well. And then, after over thirty years of faithful service, the inevitable. The mighty Zebco took its last cast. I took it apart to try and fix it, but the gear teeth were worn down to nubs, the pick-up pins deeply scored.

Sporting goods stores have plenty of rod and reel combos, far more styles, names, and sizes than I remember. I found a cheap one-piece pole with a small spincast reel, spool already filled with four pound mono. Better get two. The first rod and reel I ever bought, and not for myself.

We live five minutes from a lake that gets heavily stocked and heavily fished. It may not be the kind of fishing I grew up with, but it's great for kids. Especially once they instituted the youth mentored fishing day, opening a week before the regular season. Even then it gets crowded. Driving to the lake one April morning, we stopped at a bait shop for some red worms. It was finally time to teach my daughter, the youngest, the fine art of getting snagged on the only stick in the water for a hundred yards. I was still struggling to get her hooked up when the boys managed to get their lines tangled with one another, hooks stuck up in a tree above us.

"Dad!"

"Hang on, buddy. Okay, honey, wait here, don't swing this around or anything, okay?"

"Okay, daddy."

"Alright bud, let me see. How on earth did you manage to get this line so tangled?"

"Sorry dad."

"It's fine, just . . . Spread out a little here, okay. Cast at that fish, see him over there?"

"Dad!"

"What?"

"My worm is gone!"

"What did you do with it?"

"It fell off when I casted."

"Okay, reel in. Hang on a second, let me help your sister."

I don't know how my father ever managed. I'm outnumbered. These new reels are cheap junk, line always getting hung up. Pick up pins not picking-up. Handles falling off. I've bought six new reels in the last few years, each lasting only a season or two before the plastic mechanisms crack, the flimsy housings bend and split. Year after year.

I caved and stopped at a big-time outdoors store. No more cheap $15 combos, it was time to get serious. I spent $75 on the reel alone, and that's not even an expensive one. The salesman rang up my purchase.

"The XT? That's a good one, I've got two myself. Super-fast gear ratio, sealed bearings, anti-reverse lock. That's a quality reel!"

At least he made me feel good about my choice, I guess. It casts nice, looks cool too. Maybe in thirty years one of my kids will be teaching one of their kids with this reel. But it's still no Zebco.

# Tradition

Much has been made recently about the Pennsylvania Game Commission's vote that moved the start of rifle season to the Saturday after Thanksgiving. For the past fifty-six years - that would encompass the entire hunting career of just about any hunter who hasn't retired yet – opening day always came on the Monday after turkey and football. But Saturday?! Surely you can't be serious. Now, I've not met anyone who actually cares about the decision, mostly because I try to talk to as few people as possible. But I am able to tolerate differing opinions if I'm hearing my own voice in my own head while I read their words off a page. And after reading all the opinion pieces about the issue, I *still* don't know why anyone cares. Best I can figure is that it now means no more leaving for deer camp after work on Friday and then getting all kinds of tuned up that evening and still having a couple of days to collect yourself before you have to be a responsible firearm user. And that makes total sense to me.

But I don't want to talk about game laws and binge drinking and the logistics of taking a day off work. I want to talk about tradition. It's one of the more interesting ways to get to know a person.

"What do you do for work?"

"What's your major?"

"Where did you go to school?"

Who cares? (That's not really a question.) Like I said, I don't much enjoy talking to people. But sometimes it can be interesting, entertaining even. And never more so than when you ask about their family traditions. Hank Jr. knew as much. Why else, for our first Christmas as a married couple, did I insist on a live tree propped up in an old five-gallon bucket and held in place by bricks? Yup, tradition. All the way down to the getting mad about it toppling over and throwing tangled strings of lights against the wall. I'm not against traditions at all. Except when I am.

Opening day of rifle season used to mean driving two hours to my Grandmother's house and spending the night there. You'd bring extra clothes because the back room wasn't heated and it would be about forty degrees by bedtime. Even as a child you had to bring Tylenol because it was a given that the next morning your back would feel like a bendy straw after laying on a mattress that sagged so badly it was like sleeping in a taco shell.

Four o'clock would come pretty early for a twelve-year-old, and also for his dad, so you'd usually sleep until five. A short drive later you'd sit down to the "Hunters Welcome" breakfast, feeling a bit out of place amongst all the locals. Of course, the awkwardness didn't last long – they were already done with breakfast and were heading out into the field, silently judging you for arriving so late. Just before sunup you'd get to the rally point and plans would be made with all the other guys standing around. Dudes with names like Hambone and Dogpile, Cooter and Fat Tommy. But twelve, thirteen, fourteen-year-old you would stand silently off to the side, intimidated by the grizzled veterans and their complete disregard for decorum when it came to four letter words and impressionable children. Mostly you just felt ignored.

A few hours trying to sit still in a tree stand and seeing nothing but squirrels ultimately led to frozen toes and disappointment, but reprieve would eventually come in the form of "Well, let's wander back to the truck and see if those guys have had any luck." Sometimes there might be a little four point in the back of someone's truck, and I remember anytime I'd see that I would be jealous, not because they had a deer and I didn't, but because now they got to sit in truck with the heater running while the rest of us idiots wandered back out into the woods. On some occasions there'd be a real monster, a two-and-a-half-year-old eight point with antlers almost out to its ears, and by noon everyone from all the neighboring deer camps would know about it.

My favorite deer camp tradition had to be lunchtime. You'd get to set down the fifteen-pound rifle you'd been carrying. That's it. That's why I liked it. But there was also always a can of Dinty Moore beef stew. They didn't have the easy open lids with the pull tab on the cans then, though, so you'd dig out a pocketknife with a bent opener and try not to get gravy all over your gloves as you fabricated a little ninja star lid with enough points and sharp edges to take down a moose. If luck was really with you the Coleman stove would still have fuel in it and you'd just have to pump and prime and light it. That happened for me once. Every other time you'd just try to pour fuel from a container with an opening about an inch across into the quarter inch aperture of the stove body. Most of it would be on your gloves, of course. Scent control wasn't really a tradition then. The stove would sputter and maybe half of it would catch, but you knew your dad was waiting for you to finish so he could heat up his own lunch, so you'd give it a half-hearted stir with a little aluminum camping spoon that conducted heat better than an electric stove coil. Then you'd find a spot to sit or lean against that wasn't covered with snow or covered with soot or covered with weird, unidentifiable fungus, and you'd dig in. And goddamn wasn't that the best meal you ever ate? I still get weird pangs of affection on the rare occasion that I open a can and see those bits of fat floating around in the thin, watery gravy. I'll never not like that stew.

Spirits lifted after lunch there'd be another powwow with anyone who still hadn't tagged out, and the next plan would be made. This was the part I dreaded: the deer drive. Nowadays? I love driving deer. I love when other people drive deer to me. I've got GPS and OnX Maps (and a few more years of experience walking around in the woods). My sense of direction hates deer drives. Especially my early teenage years sense of direction. I feel like my father thought that all his knowledge of an area got passed along genetically somehow, so you'd receive your instructions like this:

"Go past the ol' chicken fightin' place about three hundred yards to where they blew up that cave where your relatives used to run counterfeit silver dollars, then go up a little rise and turn left where the dead maple tree used to be before your great grandfather cut it down. You'll come to a clearing where the deer like to cross to the West, so watch that way, down towards old Ralphie's property."

I wasn't the one driving deer, here. No, I was supposed to get out in front of everybody and they'd drive the deer to me. I'd go what I assumed was three hundred yards and wander around a little bit until I found what looked like a clearing. I had no idea which way West was, so

I'd just sit under a tree and kind of look around a bit, trying not to fall asleep. My fantasy was always the same – a huge buck walks out just a few steps away and doesn't see me and then I shoot it and it drops right there and guts itself, and my dad shows up in time to see me standing there, a triumphant killer. A killer who can now go warm up because there's no shame in it once you've punched your tag.

As a kid I only ever went out on opening day of rifle. We'd only shoot bucks. I don't really ever remember bringing any of the meat home, though I know we took it to get processed by this old-timer who had a bunch of Amish guys working for him. If anyone in our caravan managed to tag out, you'd roll up to this guy's warehouse style facility and they'd drag the deer out of your truck and if you wanted the horns they'd cut them off with a hacksaw right there in the parking lot and hand them over. I also remember when we went there to drop off a deer and he had closed up shop. Talk about traditions dying.

And that was deer season.

I cherish all those traditions and I love all those memories, but there's not much in a hunting season for me that resembles those times. My own children's experiences are certainly similar in some fundamental ways – learning how to get up early and sit still and be cold and suffer and maybe be a little intimidated by all the old guys standing around cursing – but there are plenty of differences. We go out during archery season now, an activity that's a world away from the frantic deer I grew up with. I always get all the kids a doe tag, so success rates are somewhat higher. I've started the new tradition of processing our own deer, just to feel a little more connected to the whole thing. My kids help me make up some elaborate dishes, down to roasting bones for stock. There's a cabin on the property now, no more sleeping at Grandma's house. There's running water, a refrigerator, and a fully functioning stove that has coils that heat up almost as fast as an aluminum camping spoon. But I always make sure that the pantry is stocked with a few cans of Dinty Moore beef stew.

# Pay (Selective) Attention

I've walked this path through these woods hundreds of times. The path leads from the cabin past the tractor shed and by the tall pine tree where the red squirrels hide whenever someone brings out the .22, a forty-year-old Marlin that's seen its share of pop cans, critters, and paper targets. If you turn right you'll hit the dirt road maybe a hundred yards down a gentle slope through a stand of hemlock and poplar, but if you go straight you'll get to what we've come to call "the racetrack", because at one point my uncle was big into go karts and built a racetrack for them there. You can still see the oval shape where I once rode with my oldest when he was still a toddler, precarious on my lap as we skidded around the turn at the far end, me trying to hold the wheel and him at the same time while still attempting to pass my cousin who was a far better driver. I was unsuccessful. Most everything there is covered with head high weeds and emerging pine trees now. It's a good spot to find deer beds and antler sheds if you know what signs to look for.

Arriving at the racetrack, the path splits again, and I usually turn left, following my dogs as they nose the ground. I'll stop at a tree where I have my first trail camera set up over a mock scrape. The first week after the scrape was started I got pictures of deer, turkey, raccoons, possum, one fox, a fisher, and hundreds of pictures of grass or branches waving in the wind. I've seen more videos of the tree under which I made that scrape than I can count. You'd think I'd be able to tell you what kind of tree it was. Or maybe draw a picture approximating its structure. Is it tall and straight? Branched a bunch near the bottom? Maple? Apple? Beech?

Part of the problem is that I suck at identifying trees. If the leaves are on I can pick out oak and maple, poplar, maybe even cherry. Show me a chunk of wood? Forget it. My father does this thing where he'll scratch at a piece of wood with his thumbnail and give it a sniff declaring "That's mahogany" as sure as if he's proclaiming the day of the week. We once burned a big pile of wood shavings from his workshop and it wasn't five minutes later that my uncle showed up on a four-wheeler, saying he was worried the cabin caught fire because he smelled burning walnut. I could maybe tell you if someone was burning popcorn, but I would be unable to get brand specific.

The other reason I couldn't tell you much about that tree, other than that it has a licking branch at just the right height for the bucks to rub their foreheads against, is that when I'm looking at camera footage, I don't care about the tree. I can tell you which bucks visited, what time they like to show up, how many poults the hen that lives near the racetrack was able to hatch this year. I can tell you if the wide nine point with the split brow tine got any bigger this year, and whether or not I can expect to see this old massive four point that's been spotted the last few seasons. I kinda feel like I should be able to identify that tree, though.

The path continues on, out by "the treehouse", a platform maybe eight to ten feet up with walls, windows, and a roof. A good spot to take your kids when they're just starting out hunting. A good spot to hunt from even after you've been doing it for years. Just inside the tree line is another camera setup. I know that the tree holding this camera is an apple tree, but only because I picked an apple tree on purpose. What are all the other trees? I haven't bothered to notice.

A singular focus has served me very well my whole life. Being lasered in on a specific goal has allowed me to complete many projects that otherwise would have taken more time, money, or manpower. I once went hiking with the intention of photographing snakes. I found plenty and got some impressive (to me) pictures developed. It was a rather popular hiking trail in state park near Baltimore so there was a good bit of foot traffic. I was so dialed in I could spot snakes simply by looking for a difference in the way the sun bounced off the scales, yet somehow overlooked the deer that was standing on the opposite side of the river. It was the small group of people that caught my attention, and only then because I had to detour around them as they stood in the path, watching the deer that was watching them. Selective attention is well documented (if you haven't googled "selective attention test" yet, give it a whirl), and absolutely necessary. Blocking out things our brains deem unimportant is essential to our survival, or at least kind of important in preventing us from going crazy.

I have a hard time shutting down the selective attention mechanism in my brain, though. Even if I have no specific goal in mind, I'm always trying to get to whatever the next thing is. The next chapter. The next episode. The next "thing". I'm not good at watching television programs on Netflix because I'd rather just read the recap of each available season to find out what's going on. My favorite book, that I've read dozens of times, has a few pages near the back that I've always managed to gloss over since the hero has by this point already achieved his goal. Slowing down takes practice.

This path that I follow, right around a mile and a half from start to finish, holds a galaxy of biotic interactions. Beetles lumbering beneath the undergrowth, trees and shrubs silently synthesizing sugar and oxygen, bird species that I should know by their calls but don't singing away about whatever it is they want to sing about in that particular moment. Goals are good, and so I've set one for myself – to walk the path again, this time without a focus. To experience what's there just as it is, listen to anything that's willing to be heard, and, since I can't shut it down entirely, maybe try to identify a few trees.

# Live and Unplugged

I trust a truck stop vending machine tuna sandwich more than I trust career politicians. That is to say, my political opinions are pretty much irrelevant to this story. But it was Tuesday night of the 2016 presidential election and the staff from the local paper was camped out and live broadcasting from my kitchen, so it was a bit inescapable. My wife worked for the paper at the time, and we lived close enough that when their computer system went down they were able to move the operation over to our house. The industry in general, while perhaps being objective and unbiased when it comes to writing, editing, and reporting newsworthy stories, tends to be made up of people in the moderate-to-liberal end of the political spectrum. As such, you can imagine how that night went. For the next couple days (and long after) the topic was unavoidable, brought up either gleefully or with a look of puzzled bewilderment, depending on who you thought was the good guy. The constant media saturation became much to deal with, and the annual tradition of "unplugged weekend" was born.

The idea was simple, and it's been extensively written about in everything from child behavior magazines to books about homesteading. Technology, screens specifically, can have an adverse effect on health, mood, creativity, and just about any other metric you could measure that's considered "good". Of course limiting exposure to screens doesn't require driving two hours over rutted dirt roads, but it does somehow reduce the temptation. Especially when there's no cell service. Much has been written about the benefits of reducing screen use, but it's even easier to find sources extolling the virtues of being outside. All those "good" things that screen use seems to inhibit? They all seem to be improved with even minimal exposure to natural settings. Obviously there's some overlap, and so combining those two ideas just made sense. Kind of a hybridization of "Four Arguments for the Elimination of Television" and "The Nature Fix" – if you haven't read those yet, put this down and go do that instead.

That first unplugged weekend kicked off the same way as my last three previous weekends – with getting up early, waking boy number 2, and heading out to a tree stand. Deer season was still on, and there would be plenty of time for sitting around with family being not entertained by the internet later. The difference this time was that someone let the dogs out of the cabin and it wasn't long before they tracked us down and we were busted, so it seemed like a great time to head back in. You know how commercials on TV have the mom pouring orange juice from a glass pitcher (who does that?) while bacon sizzles away and pancakes brown up all pancakedly, only to have her dick of a husband snatch up his keys, stuff a piece of toast in his face and head out the door, one arm flailing for the other sleeve of his sport coat? That's when it's a BMW commercial. If it's a commercial for pop-tarts or laxatives or whatever, then her kids come racing down the stairs because they're stupid and didn't get up in time for school so she silently hands them a bagged lunch and rolls her eyes as they run out the door. And if the commercial is for coffee then it ends with the mom smiling over her mug as the bus pulls up and her ungrateful brats disappear for seven hours and she can finally do whatever the hell it is one does when they clearly have enough time to prepare giant breakfasts that go uneaten day after day. That was our breakfast that first day, minus the rush. We had bacon. We had eggs. There might have even been hash browns. There was certainly coffee. And no one raced anywhere. We all just kind of hung out and talked. It was like living in a Norman Rockwell.

Two and a half years separate my two boys, and my daughter is over three years behind that. She and the oldest don't interact much. That inaugural weekend, the oldest was more than twice the age of the youngest. I was used to seeing them not talk or hang out. But they did then. All three kids disappeared after breakfast, "going to go play at the gravel pit", they said. The gravel pit is just a big hole in the ground where gravel was dug out for use in roadbeds or something, and then slowly filled in with old washing machines and junked bicycles until someone couldn't take it anymore and bulldozed everything under. It's even labeled "Gravel Pit" on the official USGS quadrant map. When they finally came back hours later they were covered with dirt and scratches and full of stories of cool things they had done and all the stuff they had found.

The weekend was spent playing board games, picking apples to fry up and sprinkle with cinnamon, walking the paths and old logging roads through continuously falling leaves, and reading in front of the fireplace.

It was such a success that there wasn't even discussion about doing it again. The only change was that we moved it to later in the year, to the weekend between archery and rifle season, when at least two of us wouldn't be so distracted. Safer for the dogs that way, too.

I like to keep a little record of every visit that I make up there. After getting home I'll get out a small black moleskine notebook and make notes about who was there, what the weather was like, how many times I beat my father in cribbage. And I had the kids each write a little something after that first visit. I like to go back and read it from time to time. I especially like my daughter's first entry, when she was six. It just says "It was fun picin walnuts."

My kids have since discovered pressing apple cider, building lean-to shelters, sledding down gaslines, skinny dipping in the mudhole that masquerades as a pond, getting lost in the woods, and whipping crab apples off the end of sticks. Unplugged weekend has become something we attempt two or three times a year now. Bottle rockets found their way into the mix last Fourth of July, and there's been a growing interest in shooting.

About a year ago my wife switched our cell service provider. It was more complicated than it should have been, but the end result is that I can now text her whenever I get there. You used to have to type out your message in advance and then go stand in one particular spot in the yard, push send, and wait to see that little "delivered" text pop up under your word bubble. Maybe a few hours later you'd go back out to that same spot, or, if there were clouds you'd hike ten minutes up a hillside until you had signal, and then stand there for a few minutes with your arm extended to the sky seeing if any messages had come through. There are things I like about the instant access now, like being able to see just how much time I have on the tractor until the rain starts, or not having to hold my phone up over my head simply to say "See you tomorrow, dear!" Then again, it has also become way too easy to look up the score of the game and just watch a quick highlight, to take yourself out of the moment so you can post that photo to facespace, to keep one toe in the water that you've been trying to escape. We might just leave all the phones at home this year.

# A First Time for Everything

I've only ever heard coyotes from a distance of more than a mile (I assume, I mean, how do you tell?). At any rate, they weren't a common sound, at least not close ones. I'd never heard them this close. They were less than three hundred yards away. I know this because I was standing in front of a dead doe hanging from a tree whose stomach, intestines, heart, and assorted other bits were themselves less than three hundred yards from where I stood with my 11 year old son (the heart was actually impaled on a broken off hemlock branch because I had intended on bringing it out and making a go of frying it that night, but, well, things happen.) As it was, my son and I listened to the yipping of what sounded like a dozen coyotes but was likely no more than two or three wolfing down (coyoteing down?) the ridiculous bounty that they had happened upon.

It wasn't my son's first doe, nor even his second, but what made it special was that it was the first one he recovered. I know, what kind of hunter (or hunter's father) doesn't recover their deer? I'd like to plead bad luck and my own relative ignorance for the lack of recovery, so that's what I'm going to do. Hunting with my son now was not like it was for me when I was his age. There were similarities, of course. This doe was recovered no more than five hundred yards from where I recovered my own first deer, a spindly little 5 point, nearly thirty years earlier, my own father showing me how to dress it out much as I had just finished doing for my son. Then, though, we were rifle hunting over wide open fields. A deer shot from a tree stand could be watched as it ran fifty or a hundred yards and then collapsed, recovery was rarely difficult.

My son, Mac, shot his first doe the year before. We were sitting in two folding chairs in high grass next to a field of clover. No hunting blind, no scent killer, no distressed fawn calls, just us and a crossbow. This is the part where I'm supposed to say what model it was and what bolts and broadheads we were using, but really, who cares? Maybe people do, but I always gloss over those parts when reading hunting stories. It's like when people spend a paragraph detailing the protagonist's clothing. I'd rather spend my time writing about what I'm not going to write about, apparently. She (the doe, not my son), came out no more than ten yards to our left. I tried to make sure he (my son, not the doe) was settled and lined up, and also still awake. Something about our appearance there in the grass alarmed her, but only enough to drive her off for a few minutes. After a bit of huffing and stomping, she soon chanced to come back into the field again, approaching from the same spot. I tried to film it with my phone, thinking it would make a cool slow motion video (and something we could refer to if we needed to look at shot placement), but of course I was so excited that the video showed her walking into and then out of the frame while I never moved the camera. Mac took the shot, the doe kicked and then turned and ran straight at us, veering off no more than six feet from where we sat. She was close enough for me to smell her, and I still swear that I heard her crash in the woods only a little ways away. The video ends with me moving the camera to Mac's face and him asking excitedly "Did I get her?"

"You sure did, buddy!" I can be heard saying as the camera cuts out. Sorry, Mac, my bad. Now, I wasn't wrong – he got that deer, a perfect shot placement that was confirmed when I found the carcass two weeks later. After looking for an hour and not finding her where we expected, I, my son, and my father went to a nearby Perkins for dinner in order to let some time pass in case it was warranted. Of course two of the three of us weren't very hungry. We then stopped at a Wal-Mart to buy a three-function flashlight from a lady that really seemed like she'd rather be cleaning a public port-a-john than behind the counter dealing with the kind of people who show up at Wal-Mart at 10:30 at night dressed in camouflage. It had a regular LED white light, which was admittedly bright enough to blind alien spacecraft, a red light which, well I don't know what that was for, and a purplish setting that was supposed to make blood stand out. Returning back to the spot where we lost track of my son's deer, we lit up that flashlight. I guess I expected it to make the blood trail glow or something, but really it was only good for pointing out spots that were wet – they'd kind of shine with a black-ish glow. Of course, it had started raining slightly so everything had splatters of water all over it and the light ultimately proved useless. We didn't recover the deer soon enough to make use of the meat, but I think my son still has fond memories of wandering through the woods at 11:30 at night trying to differentiate between pinprick sized drops of blood and the pinprick sized flecks of autumn-induced red that had already begun to form on the leaves that littered the forest floor.

His second deer was the same story except that this one required extraordinary patience on his part. We had decided that spending money on seeds and investing time to plant those seeds in order to grow crops to feed deer was a good idea, but we didn't want them reaping the bounty at just any old time. Consequently, we had to spend a weekend cutting down poplar trees in order to make fenceposts so we could keep the deer out of our turnips until *we* decided they could have them. In hindsight, what we spent in terms of both time and money we could have probably bought a half a cow that would have lasted us a whole year, but that's not really the point, is it? We left that fence up so long that by the time we tried to hunt from a blind on one side of the food plot, the tops of the turnips had grown so high you couldn't see the deer when they approached from the other side. This is how my son and I ended up spending over an hour watching a doe not thirty yards away work her way through a never-ending salad bar. Based on the photo data I still have on my phone, that doe walked out into the high greens at 4:47 October 21st, 2017. By the time she presented a shot (which I managed to get on film this time), it was after six o'clock. There was the shot (him), the jump (the deer), the nervous exhale of breath (him), the shaking from the adrenaline dump (both of us). Then the rain came. Before we even managed to make it out of the blind the rain had not only washed away any hope of a blood trail, it had also smashed all the vegetation down to a point where it seemed as though fifty deer had run through. Not that it made a difference, it was now too dark to see anything but our feet anyways. We wandered blindly through waist high thorns until neither him nor I could keep it up. We drove the two hours home the next morning, both dejected. The following week we, of course, found his doe piled up under a tree that we had both walked past at least three times. The fact that it was another perfect shot was of little consolation.

This time, though, this time ended with us looking at a deer hanging from a tree while coyotes chorused almost uncomfortably close. This time he got to track his deer, a third perfect shot, fifty yards through tall pines with an open understory. The range of emotions that crossed his face when he realized that he had a) shot a deer, b) successfully tracked and recovered that deer, and then c) took the life of that deer, was like watching a slightly tragic yet ultimately happy movie take place over only a couple of seconds.

The field dressing work done, we entered into new territory for the both of us. This was the year, I had decided, that I would butcher and process my own deer rather than paying someone else to do what humans had been doing for themselves since the dawn of man. I had already purchased a vacuum sealer and meat grinder, as well as a top of the line dehydrator that was supposedly great for making venison jerky. I was prepared for this. I had watched countless YouTube videos on the subject (okay, like three videos, but I watched each one at least twice. That one where the Scottish guy breaks down a deer in like less than a minute? Crazy.) I'd read books on butchering deer (all right, books that had small sections devoted to butchering deer), listened to podcasts about deer processing - but learn by doing, right? I wanted to be more connected to the whole process, because apparently I hate grocery stores and convenience.

The coyotes are yipping, the doe carcass is slowly spinning around on a rope, refusing to stay in one spot, I'm trying not to lose my patience with my son (POINT THE DAMN FLASHLIGHT SO I CAN SEE WHAT I'M DOING!), he's tripping over broken cinder blocks because they happened to be beneath the closest branch I could find on which to hang a deer. Let's just fast forward that unpleasantness to the point where we've got the deer skinned and quartered. So, more hours later than I'd like to admit, we've got four deer legs, some backstraps, and some tenderloins neatly stacked, though maybe covered in hair and dirt and bugs, on the front porch of the cabin. At least there were porch lights.

The cabin had only been there for the last six years, though it felt as though it had always been part of the landscape. When I hunted this property, in the family for long enough that I don't know when it first became "Eastman Property", there had been a dirt roofed dugout like shelter. I'm sure my own father would tell me I'm wrong and that it didn't have a dirt roof or that it was two stories tall or paneled in old growth redwood, but my memories as a child paint it as something dug into a hillside with large floor to ceiling glass window/sliding door combinations. Not fancy at all, mind you, more like the kind of place you would take a kidnapping victim if you didn't care what they thought about how you lived. I remember huddling over a sputtering Coleman stove heating up cans of soup and beef stew every opening Monday of deer season in that place, next to some rusted out bedsprings and what looked like bloodstains on the cement foundation. It also seemed much colder then.

Now? You ever see those expectation vs reality photos people do when they make a cake or build a shoe tree they found on Pinterest? The cabin my father built is the "expectation" picture. It's nicer than any house I've ever lived in, including the one he and my mother still share. Giant, high ceilinged great room, big fireplace, custom woodwork throughout – I'm a little upset he hadn't built it when I was younger and needed a place to take girls that I wanted to impress. Back before we were married, my own wife had to make do with a tent at the bottom of the field that the cabin overlooks. A field that was of course flooded because why wouldn't it be raining when I was trying to press my luck? All this is to say that the cabin feels as much a part of the landscape as the deer, trees, chittering squirrels, and gently winding gravel drive.

The butchering surface was supposed to be a big stainless-steel table, the kind you get from a restaurant auction, except that I got outbid on Every. Single. One. As it was, the butcher block was a big chunk of wood countertop from Ikea that was left over from a kitchen renovation. My son alternately watched and dozed as I tried to find the muscle seams as effortlessly as the guys I had seen do it in videos. By the end of the night, I'd managed to turn a hundred or so pounds of muscle, bone, and hide into just over fifty pounds of slightly tormented looking meat and one ridiculously deep cut on my finger. Everyone is always like "DuLL kNiVes aRe MoRE DaNGeRous ThAn SHarP OnEs!" Well, I'd hate to run into a dull one then, because mine was sharp as shit and it cut through my finger like a hot wire through soft cheese. We vacuum sealed the large cuts and put the grind pile into gallon sized freezer bags and hauled the lot home in coolers the following day. Over the next few months we made piles of jerky, lots of hamburgers, homemade bone broth, two really impressive meals of reverse seared backstraps, and one memorable experiment in making osso bucco where my son's friends stayed for dinner and couldn't get enough.

We're now getting things organized for the upcoming season - planting more, fencing more, paying more attention to what's happening on the land, getting my daughter set up to follow her brother. It sounds goofy to say it this way, but it's been ten months since my son became a "provider" for his family. You could see the pride on his face when we'd all sit down to dinner and I'd say "The steak for these fajitas came from the deer you shot." He was proud, and I was proud of him.

# Getting Sappy

**M**aple syrup is pretty good. I mean, I'm not crossing state lines to make sure I get the best stuff or anything, but I can appreciate a healthy pour of real syrup over a stack of pancakes. Not that I'm crazy about pancakes, I'm definitely more of a hash browns and bacon kind of guy, but it has a place in my refrigerator, and I care enough to get the real stuff. None of that cheap, lying "maple flavored" corn syrup. I guess I like maple syrup just enough to be offended by the likes of Mrs. Butterworth or Log Cabin. Real maple syrup retails for a little less than $1 an ounce, give or take. A quick scan online finds some for as much as $2.30 an ounce (if it's that important to you that your syrup has aged for ten years in a whiskey barrel that's visited weekly by wailing virgins, then have at it, I guess?)

Assuming climate change doesn't turn all our sugar maples into saguaros, and assuming I can manage to achieve a somewhat average life span (I've got another 30 years in me, right?), I imagine that I'd require maybe a gallon of maple syrup to see me through to the end of my days. At just under a dollar an ounce, that comes out to about one hundred and fifteen dollars. One gallon. One hundred and fifteen dollars. That would shepherd me on to the end of my Earthly tenure, even leaving me enough syrup to spike the baked beans once in a while. That's all a long way of saying that, while I like maple syrup, I probably wouldn't be too troubled if it became inaccessible. And that? That makes my recent endeavor seem as ridiculous as maple flavored sugar water.

At some point, perhaps in an alcoholic stupor, I was hit with the idea that I should take a crack at making my own maple syrup. After all, I've got maple trees, right? And if a bunch of three-toothed Appalachian hillfolk can figure it out, surely I'd be the Walter White of sweet tree juice. I read forums about the virtues of plastic vs aluminum spiles, the benefits of a filter press, the rabid hatred of something called "sugar sand." I watched people bore holes in trees with antique hand drills, pour sap through old t-shirts, use computerized systems to alert them when their product met the perfect specific gravity. Everyone had advice on what made the perfect maple syrup.

"You don't tap the trees until you hear the spring song of the warbling red throat."

"Tap your maples – sugar and red, but not silver – when the daytime temperatures exceed 41°F and the overnight lows drop to below freezing."

"If the wooly bear caterpillar has thicker brown stripes than black, tap your trees on the next odd numbered Tuesday after the first snowfall over three inches. . ."

And that advice all came from just one guy.

So it ended up that I spent $136.58 (plus tax) on spiles, T-junctions, filters, and tubing, and another $21 on a case of Yuengling, and headed up to the property in early February to make my maple fortune.

Making a maple fortune by yourself is a lonely business, so I invited a few other people, who obviously had nothing better to do, to make the drive up to a cold cabin in order to spend a weekend recovering from hangovers and doing manual labor.

A Friday evening arrival meant it was too dark to do any serious maple work, so I set my sights on doing a bunch of fermented grain work instead. (Add $20 lost in a poker game to the running total, if you're keeping score.) But Saturday, now Saturday was a day for some serious work. I suppose that's why one of our crew decided it would be a good time to bail out and head home. Turns out he's the smart one. Those of us that remained set about the business of sweet, sweet, maple tapping. Only we didn't, at least not yet, because if we were going to boil up gallons and gallons of sap, we'd need fuel. So we dragged our chainsaws and headaches out to the woods to look for some promising trees, and began cutting. I took a break to vomit a couple times, and before you could say "this is a stupid idea," we had ourselves a pile of firewood. Unfortunately, we'd need to get about two dozen more piles of firewood if we were going to have enough to boil all the sap we were sure we'd collect.

A little explanation of the maple syrup making process, in case you're unfamiliar. To make a gallon of maple syrup – which again, would cost maybe $115 or so, and would last me the rest of my life – it requires forty gallons of maple sap. The sap is thin, like water, and must be filtered (to get rid of all the debris and bugs that find their way in), and then boiled for a month or so to reduce it down to the viscosity of maple syrup. There are actual people who took actual time to make regulations concerning what can and cannot be called "maple syrup." I'll just leave this here:

[Code of Federal Regulations]

[Title 21, Volume 2]

[Revised as of April 1, 2019]

[CITE: 21CFR168.140]

TITLE 21 – FOOD AND DRUGS

CHAPTER I – FOOD AND DRUG ADMINISTRATION

DEPARTMENT OF HEALTH AND HUMAN SERVICES

SUBCHAPTER B – FOOD FOR HUMAN CONSUMPTION

PART 168 – SWEETENERS AND TABLE SIRUPS

Subpart B – Requirements for Specific Standardized Sweeteners and Table Sirups

Sec. 168.140 Maple sirup

(a) Maple sirup is the liquid food derived by concentration and heat treatment of the sap of the maple tree (Acer) or by solution in water of maple sugar (mapel concrete) made from such sap. It contains not less than 66 percent by weight of soluble solids derived solely from such sap. The concentration may be adjusted with or without added water. It may contain one or more of the optional ingredients provided for in paragraph (b) of this section. All ingredients from which the food is fabricated shall be safe and suitable.

(b) The optional ingredients that may be used in maple sirup are:

    (1) Salt.

    (2) Chemical preservatives.

    (3) Defoaming agents.

(c) The name of the food is "Maple sirup". Alternatively, the word "sirup" may be spelled "syrup".

(d) Label declaration. Each of the ingredients used in the food shall be declared on the label as required by the applicable sections of parts 101 and 130 of this chapter.

[42 FR 14479, Mar. 15, 1977, as amended at 58 FR 2896, Jan. 6. 1993]

So it's all very official and complex, and I'm sure that the old-time Vermonters had some quaint system to determine when their product had reached the perfect consistency.

"Can it form a sheen on the back of a three-day-old mule's hoof? Now THAT'S syrup!"

So after cutting down half the dead trees in the forest and hauling them back to the cabin and stacking them by the fire pit, we were ready to begin the real work. We were going to tap some trees. Being the super savvy woodsman I am, I knew what maple trees looked like. I'd even taken the time to watch a tutorial on differentiating between silver, red, and sugar maples. Drill in hand, I strode out confidently to look for our first victim. I was going to tap that tree so good I'd end up an internet star.

It turns out that using the shape of a maple leaf to identify the tree is a great idea for about 7 months of the year. February isn't one of those months. But never fear, more capable people were along and they could point out a maple tree by . . . the bark, I think? The way the branches . . . branched? At any rate, we found some maples and went to town. I read that the ideal depth for drilling a tap hole was an inch and a half. I scrounged up a couple of 5/16" drill bits and wrapped a line of tape to indicate the correct depth. All that was left was to drill the hole.

"What the hell are you doing? You can't drill on a downward angle you moron! How's the sap going to flow?"

"Sorry, dad."

"No, no, no, drill on the southeastern side of the tree, where the sun will hit!"

"You... you mean over ... here?"

"Does that look like southeast to you!"

"Uh . . ."

"Gimme that!"

And of course, the drill bit was dull, and that somehow (of course) made me more of an idiot.

So, being a disappointment to the old man aside, we succeeded in injuring some trees and running IV lines to a few large barrels where we'd collect our liquid gold. It was about this time that my uncle showed up, out for a ride on his four-wheeler. I knew he was laughing even before he turned off his ATV.

"The hell you got all this shit strung up through the woods for? The deer are just gonna run right through it!"

He was really enjoying this.

What followed was a brief discussion about wasting time and how there exist such things as grocery stores where you can buy maple syrup for much less than what I had already invested and we all had a good laugh and I didn't feel at all like I'd wasted a weekend haha etc. etc.

But really, I didn't see it as a waste. And I think it comes down to this: I don't need to know how to make maple syrup. My kids probably won't need to know how to make maple syrup. But their kids? Their grandkids? Who can say?

Things should start warming up in the next few weeks, and, if I can believe anything on the internet, the sap should start flowing. Sometime soon I'll make the trip up there again with my kids, and we'll spend a weekend boiling sap. Maybe we'll have collected a gallon, maybe forty. Either way, each log we throw on the fire will have the memory of that cold February weekend. And even if we manage just a pint of syrup, you can bet your ass it'll taste better than any that we've ever had. I bet it'll be worth about $136.58 an ounce.

# Social Distance and the American Sportsman

There's a fiercely independent, oftentimes antagonistic streak that flows through the blood of the American sportsman. A "get off my lawn!" merit badge, awarded to those demonstrating mastery of cantankerousness. This streak can cause us to see society as a villain to be shunned in pursuit of social distance. Aloneness, as opposed to loneliness, is something to be sought after, a frequently elusive grail in a world of seven billion.

Trout season was winding down. I had made it a goal to fish thirty times that year. This trip marked day number eight, and I don't think I even broke double digits before archery season rolled around. That is to say, this trip marked the final eleven or twelve percent of my fishing season. If you can only make it out eight times a year, each trip is special.

Which is why it's so especially awful when it goes poorly. And not because of the fish.

"Oh hey, yeah, he's a beaut. I caught one like that with my nephew a couple weeks back. You know where they stock up by the upper bridge, there's a hole up there that always holds a couple lunkers like that. But you gotta get 'em before that parking lot fills up or you can't even get close."

I about dropped my fish, my net, and my pole in the water, mostly because I had no idea who was talking. Somehow, with me standing out in the middle of the creek, green water up to my waist, this guy – I always think of guys like this as yahoos, but it's pronounced YAY-hoos – snuck up on me and about gave me a heart attack. You know the guy - talks too loud, stands too close, acts too friendly. At least a heart attack would have saved me having to listen to him any longer.

I nodded to act like I cared about him or his nephew. That should have been the end of it. He should have taken the hint and continued on downstream, or upstream, or whichever direction he was heading before he materialized from the ether to ruin the glory that was the last fish I caught for the year.

"Say, whatchya got on? A Panther Martin? Here, you gotta try one of these little spoons I got. Guy I work with's brother makes 'em in his garage. Or it might be his dad. Yeah, no wait, it's his brother because he told me how they used to fish with 'em back when they was kids. These things crush 'em."

Let's just ignore that I was catching them with spinners all morning. Sure, buddy. Let me use your yogurt lid trout slayer.

Anyone who has hunted public land, fished public waters, or just generally been a member of the public, knows that generally members of the public suck. Some places are made specifically to contain the suck that is the public. Shopping malls, highways, cities – all acceptable places for the public to suck. But in the middle of a trout stream? I can't relax while fishing if there's even another angler in sight, so when you stick one right up next to me, especially when the rest of the stream is empty? Oh man.

My spot ruined, I let him have the stream to himself. I'd drive a few miles to another spot and seek some solitude there. I got there to find two vehicles pulled off on the shoulder, and that was two too many. I headed home instead.

Social distancing, then, should be a no-brainer for an outdoorsman. The Covid-19 pandemic in full swing, social media feeds became littered with fat lipped bass held against picturesque lake backdrops and panoramic views of Wyoming trout streams. Subtitles about #socialdistancing, all very self-congratulatory, populated feeds and timelines across all platforms.

But it's not from all of society that we seek isolation and distance. Just the part of society we don't count among "our" group. Hunting and fishing may be solitary activities much of the time, but the end of the day return to camp brings with it a social reunion. Stories about the day's successes and mishaps are no fun when told to yourself, and if you can't complain, gripe, or brag about it, did it really happen? As they say, there are two kinds of hunting and fishing folks – those that are in your party, and assholes.

Trout season is fast approaching, though what kind of season it will be remains to be seen. Maybe the infections will taper off. Maybe I'll be able to go out. If I catch a big one, I'll be sure to post it on social media for everyone to see.

# Does the Pope Wear a Funny Hat?

A Google search for "How to shit in the woods" turns up over thirty-six million results, one being a book by the very same name. YouTube offers countless videos (Videos? Really?), none of which I watched, that I suppose explain technique or . . . something. It turns out one of the main reasons my wife was not keen on visiting the property early on was because of the lack of something more dignified than a hole dug in the ground with a boot heel.

I don't recall my first time. I'm sure it was on a canoe trip somewhere, it might have even been in Canada. What I do know is that I certainly never received any individualized instruction in the matter. My high school had a canoe club, housed under the umbrella of what was once referred to as "Lifetime Activities" - outdoor pursuits like rock climbing, backpacking, and caving. The program has long since shut down, more from increasing liability and litigiousness than decreasing interest, but that's another essay for another day.

One of the more important jobs on each outdoor trip was the construction of the "KYBO", short for Keep Your Bowels Open, because nothing could ruin a good canoe trip faster than being backed up on the back end. A typical kybo was a platform constructed log cabin style over a hole and topped with an old toilet seat. A tarp or two would be strung up around the structure to offer the sitter some measure of privacy. The canoe club kept a roll of toilet paper in a bright orange holder, called the kybo key, which would be hung in a conspicuous location. If the kybo key was missing, you knew not to head back in the direction of the tarp. It was a good system for a public high school club with equal numbers of girls and boys. Of course, the conspicuous location for the kybo key was usually by the main camp tarp, often set up over the cooking area, and if you walked up and grabbed the key within sight of anyone else, you could be sure that you'd hear sing-song shouts of "We know what you're doing!" while you were attending to your needs, followed up with "Everything come out okay?" upon your return.

On one particular trip, those in charge of the kybo setup got a little adventurous and hung the toilet seat from a tree branch, so that it functioned more like a swing. This presented a problem of course, as you couldn't dig a hole big enough to cover all the potential area of trajectory. The brilliant solution was to duct tape a garbage bag to the underside of the toilet seat. Shall I paint you a picture? To my knowledge, the "swinging kybo" was a one hit wonder. I spent a couple years working for a kayak instruction school along a popular eastern river. The camp house had running water but toilet facilities were limited to porta-johns. A great gag was to wait until one of your buddies went into one and then you'd drive your vehicle up in front of it to block them in. Turns out when you don't hit the brakes you knock the whole thing over and suddenly you have one less friend. A swinging kybo ends much the same way.

Popping a squat in the woods is something that humans have been doing for a hundred thousand years. Animals far dumber than us seem to have it figured out, and they somehow seem to be cleaner about it too. The problem for us, I'm convinced, is pants. In the early days of the cabin's construction, before running water, there was an honest to god outhouse. I don't think it had a crescent moon carved into the door, but it would not have been out of place in a made for TV pioneer miniseries. But where once there was a functioning outhouse, there now existed a few boards consumed by a grown-over tangle of weeds, branches, and poison ivy. With the outhouse out of commission, the alternative was simply to find a spot and do your thing. Now pants aren't a problem when there's a place to sit, but when there's not? I told my oldest son, probably four years old at the time, just pull 'em down and have at it. There's a reason we gave him the nickname "Captain Literal." As you can imagine, he then asked, in the language of a four-year-old of course, how best to deal with the shit that had inevitably collected in the pants the he was now waddling around in. That was all that it took.

I found a folding chair, removed the plastic seat, and replaced it with an old toilet seat that I had kept for the same reason you keep dead batteries and obsolete auxiliary cables – because you just never know. I carved out a path into a dense poplar thicket with a machete and then dug a hole, chopping through roots as I went. The chair was placed over the hole, and I made sure to leave a convenient branch that would hold a roll of toilet paper at the perfect angle. This was paradise! You could sit comfortably and in total privacy, serenaded by the music of the finches and orioles during the day, the tree frogs and peepers in the evening, and the easy sighing of the branches in a gentle breeze. I bet my wife couldn't wait to come up and try it out now. She'd probably never leave.

As it turns out, mosquitos are bitches. And if you could pick anywhere that you didn't want to have a welt, that whole general area is maybe second only to "directly on the eyeball." My attempts to lure my wife into the great outdoors with the promise of spa level bowel relaxation thus thwarted, I turned my attention to the construction of a proper throne room. It didn't take long - not that I had much to do with making it happen. I suspect that my father was trying similarly to whittle down the excuses that my mother could give for not making the trip up.

"Okay dear, it's finally ready!"

I was excited, and now there was no way she could wriggle out of visiting the cabin.

"There's no door?"

Three walls, a floor and a ceiling. And even most of another wall! Apparently five planar surfaces still were not sufficient. The door was installed soon after.

My wife now visits from time to time, and I'll admit that I do prefer this more conventional setup. There's no searching for the perfect downed tree to lean against, no shoveling of dirt, and there are very few mosquitos inside the cabin. Maybe one day I'll jump on the bidet bandwagon, or maybe get a toilet with a heated seat that plays easy listening music. It's still tough to beat the freedom of pissing outside, though.

# The Difficulty of Living Simply

The desire for a simpler life strikes me as a pursuit reserved primarily for those who have been overindulged, spoiled, or otherwise pampered. After all, the urge to downgrade and divest doesn't make sense without some prior degree of excess. Now, spoiled and pampered are not words I particularly like used to describe myself, and I can already hear the sound of hunters, anglers, and backpackers snapping this book closed and using it to kindle their cooking fires. Who relishes the idea of material deprivation in the backcountry, escaping from the clamor of crowded cities, and a reprieve from idiot neighbors, idiot coworkers, and idiot drivers more than the men and women of the outdoors? We're not pampered, we're tough and self-reliant! True, but I wouldn't need to simplify if I didn't already have more than I needed, would I? I count "simple" here to mean more than just uncomplex. A simple life, for me, means focusing on the essentials and doing things yourself, for yourself. A return to "simpler" times often means more work in the long run, and if you're not cautious, a pursuit of a simple life might just have the opposite effect.

When I first moved out at the age of eighteen to attend college, I drove an '88 Ford Ranger pickup, longbed. I had a suitcase of clothes, and two orange milk crates containing a couple pairs of boots, a sleeping bag, a compact stereo, an alarm clock, and - while I don't specifically remember – there were probably some school supplies. And a toothbrush, I hope. I could load everything in the bed and still have room to sleep comfortably alongside. When I left four years later to start my first real person job, I had added a guitar, amplifier, swivel chair, a houseplant, some cooking utensils and dishes, two forks, a spoon, and a nicotine addiction. I also brought along the twin bed I had been sleeping on since Jimmy Carter was in office. By necessity, I began adding more things – work clothes, a toilet plunger, a dining room table. These things are to be expected.

The accumulation continued the way a snowball will increase in size as it rolls down a slope, inevitably packing on volume. Having a wife means having real furniture, and having small children means having enough plastic junk to conceivably lose one of said children for multiple hours, buried in Legos and Playmobil pirates by his brother in the playpen as a heart stopping prank. There were also 19 boxes of books. Thus encumbered, the move to Pennsylvania required multiple trips and the rental of a truck larger than I was comfortable piloting. After twelve years in our current house, I now have a two-car garage I can't open for fear of causing catastrophic collapse (when someone calls asking if you want some free canoes, it would be an insult to refuse.) My life has become cluttered and complicated and in danger of being buried by a landslide of accumulated odds and ends. A simpler, more natural life becomes more appealing by the day.

My idea of living more simply/naturally has begun to focus on simplifying food. I suspect that's a driving factor for many hunters. If you ever decide to wade through an ingredients list on something that comes wrapped in plastic, a graduate level understanding of Latin prefixes might be a good starting point. Food has become complex and scientific, and god damn have they done a job of making it taste good. But all the chemistry has to come at a cost. (I feel compelled to explain here that I'm not anti-science in any way. I understand the value that genetic modification has on increasing crop yields and improving things like drought tolerance and vitamin content, the role of preservatives in making products last, etc. I get it, and I'm glad it's there, and yet ...)

Hunting, while still about tradition and time spent in nature, has, for me, taken on a primary role as a way to provide while being in control of the entire process, from bowshot to butchering to braised backstrap dinner. Being in control, of course, meant adding some necessities to the mix. I suppose I could have gotten away without buying a gambrel, in fact I've skinned and quartered a few deer without one, but here we are. A better skinning knife was required, as was a better cutting surface. I'd need a bigger cooler if I was going to transport all the meat back to my house for final processing, and damned if that didn't mean the purchase of a dehydrator, vacuum sealer plus bags, a sausage stuffer, an electric smoker, meat grinder, a bag taper and tape rolls for packing ground meat, and a 20 quart stockpot I could use for making my own stock. I also spent twenty bucks at a local butcher for some of the pig fat he didn't need. And everyone knows if you want to sear backstrap you've got to use cast iron, so throw a couple of those pans in there as well. This thing has gotten expensive, both in terms of dollars and in the physical space required to house everything.

Living simply, living naturally, and living close to the Earth are sentiments that have gained a good deal of traction lately. I think it's because, at least for me, we're finally now well off enough to be able to consider them. I read an article by someone who churned their own butter as a hobby. I wonder what early settlers would make of that, knowing that someone had enough spare time to turn chores into hobbies. I imagine it would be like someone a hundred years from now explaining how they vacuumed their floors or folded laundry for entertainment. Why do it yourself when you can have a machine do it for you? I guess because you can.

I've decided that it would be a good idea to make a dedicated space for all my accumulated "making food" stuff in the basement. That space is an old coal cellar that looks like it will be the perfect place to house everything, with enough room left over for canning shelves. Of course, to make full use of it and journey further down the road of self-sufficiency, I just need to buy a pressure canner, some quart jars and pint jars with bands and lids, a jar lifter, a book or two on how best to preserve different types of food, various vegetable seeds, potting soil, fencing to keep critters out of the garden that I'll inevitably be constructing . . .

# Intermission

"Why does my dog always roll in deer shit?" I wondered, while shopping online for a thirty-five-dollar bottle of doe urine.

# Hunting 'Entertainment'

There's a thing that exists called the hunting industry. Years ago, this industry encompassed firearms and boots and bullets, and maybe a specialty publication like Field and Stream. Today's industry has grown to include biome-specific clothing and camouflage, cover scents, ozone generating devices, food plot mixes, decoys . . . and television. There are bona fide hunting celebrities whose names are synonymous with outdoor adventures, sponsored hunts, and cable tv marketing. I'm surprised there's not a *famous hunter's name here* Frozen Breakfast Burrito. Hell, maybe there is.

Now I don't want it to sound like I'm dogging on these guys or that I'm bitter and jealous of their success. I mean, I am jealous of their success. Imagine getting paid to do what others strive for years to experience. But I don't wish ill upon them or begrudge what they've accomplished. The collection of hunting celebrities has had tremendous overall positive impacts on all aspects of hunting – access, acceptance, recruitment. I think my beef – and this is entirely a "me" thing here – is in how different hunting is when it has to be distilled into a thirty to sixty-minute show. If you're a hunter, you have some idea of all the things that happen that they don't televise. But for someone who forms their opinions of hunting by watching one of these shows? For the most part, I think of these programs as "Men Whispering in Trees" television. There tends to be a lot of focus on what buck they're after, what they named it, how many years they've been following it, how many years' worth of antler sheds they've accumulated. Here's the formula:

Close up shot of washing hunting clothes in specially formulated scent-free detergent (ProTip, store brand scent free stuff does the same thing at half the cost.)

Wide angle shot of loading Rubbermaid containers into the bed of a pickup truck.

Truck door slams, sounds of key in the ignition.

View out the truck window while driving. Add a few seconds of stopping for coffee if the drive takes longer than nine minutes.

More door slamming, more whispering "Allright everybody, it's about five o'clock in the A.M. and we've reached the spot, we're gonna go ahead and get ready to head back into the woods."

Montage of spraying scent eliminator over clothing, boots, backpacks, bows, rifles, camera gear, ham sandwiches, etc.

Low angle shot of walking to the tree stand, bonus points if the camera lens passes through the tall grass.

Now the real quality shows will include some drone footage here, hovering high above the host as he either continues walking or begins climbing his tree.

There's a brief morning interview period where the host will lay out the hunting strategy, maybe give a little lesson on the history of the buck he's after. More bonus points if he stops mid-sentence, holds up one finger, and squints into the distance towards the sound of a red squirrel.

A little bit of sunrise time lapse, some B-roll of a bird or some shit that's decidedly not what he's after, and then...

Bum-Bum. Ba-Da Dum-Bum. That's right, cue the drums soundtrack. That's how you know there's supposed to be tension, and that you should start paying close attention.

There's five minutes of footage of a dandy buck working the edge of a cornfield, inching ever closer. Some shaky footage from the secondary camera gives another view of the action. Once in range, the host gives a doe bleat, sounding kind of like someone sneezing through a kazoo, and then -

The drumming stops. That's how you know he's about to take the shot, like the calm before the storm. A short exhale, zoom in on the subject, and then the *thwock* of an arrow release or the flat crack of a gunshot. A bit of crashing through the underbrush, zoom out for the chase shot, close in tight on the host while we wait for his reaction . . .

"Yeah baby! SMOKED IM! Woo!"

A fist pump, resume electric guitar riff, bro-fist with the camera man. Then the summary of everything that just happened.

"I didn't know if we'd be able to get it done today, but he came out at eighty yards and worked this field edge just like we'd seen him do before. I was a little worried he'd get distracted by that doe over there, but he just kept right on coming on a string. I heard him pile up across the creek bed, let's go."

Then comes the blood trailing footage. It has to be dark now, like past 10:00 PM. Find the arrow and inspect it for blood. Give it a sniff, check for bubbles. Close up on some bent and broken weeds with blood on them, point to some blood on the ground in the beam of a flashlight, lots of heavy breathing. "There he is!"

Cut to the host grip and grin, wresting the buck's head into position. Take time to run your hands along the antlers and pass your fingers through the fur, thank the deer for its life if you're really feeling hammy.

I don't know, watching Rodney-Bobby grin around tobacco juice and hoot and holler about his buck just turns me off. Maybe because that's where it usually ends. What about what happens after the shot and the recovery? What about hunts that are unsuccessful? I'm interested in the hunt, sure, but I also want to know how you're going to butcher your kill. More important than that, what kind of dinners are you going to prepare? Now before you point out that there's a very famous hunting show that focuses very heavily on that specific thing, yeah, I know. I've watched every episode eight or ten times. I don't have a bad word to say in that regard. Because that's the one show that makes hunting about more than just the kill. But that seems to be a rarity.

Again, I don't want to make it sound as though I dislike the work these guys are doing. It's just so foreign to my experience, and I think it's colored my view of what I should expect out of hunting. I tried filming hunts a couple of times, not to put online or anything, just as something to try, seeing as how everyone else was doing it. I tried to film a hunt where my son shot a doe. I was so invested in the action that I completely forgot that I had to move the camera and subsequently missed the shot. I later tried to film myself, a little more successfully this time. I didn't whisper to the camera or anything, but I had it mounted up and pointed towards the action. I had to shift the camera position a little bit to keep the deer in frame, which meant that instead of shooting it in the perfect position, I took a shot that was maybe not as great as it could have been.

I touched off a round when I judged the deer to be in the perfect position for a good camera view. Clean hit. My immediate reaction - check the footage. Did I capture it? Did it look cool? Could I maybe put it on YouTube after all?

I was more worried about the filming than I was about the hunting, and that took something away from the experience. My deer was now a commodity to be displayed. The measure of the experience would now be colored by what others thought of the footage I had taken. Would they think it was as cool as I did? Did I have some kind of new bragging rights since I preserved the shot on film? I think I expected it to make my hunt more meaningful when it ended up feeling like I had lost some kind of connection with the process. It wasn't just me and the animal anymore, even if no one else ever viewed the footage.

I think I'd trust the hunting media more if a few more hosts walked away empty handed. If a few more hosts expressed regret over a bad shot or a botched opportunity. Not every hunting story needs to end with triumph or redemption. Sometimes you just get beat, and that's a story worth telling.

# What Would John James Audubon Do?

W hat's the best bird out there? It's a dumb question. It has no merit, no standard, no objectivity. Yet, some birds are better than others, right? An eastern bluebird is better than a blue jay, red-tailed hawks are better than turkey vultures, and everything is better than a house sparrow. My first thought is that it's based simply on ubiquity. Goldfinches, cardinals, blue jays – among the most brightly colored of the local birds, surpassed only by the indigo bunting and Baltimore oriole – are a dime a dozen. A dime every two dozen at that.

Exotic things are exciting things. You don't notice the Honda Civic, but the Bentley catches your eye. But there has to be more to it than that. I don't know if I've ever seen a chipping sparrow. I don't even know if a chipping sparrow is real or something I just now made up, either way I certainly don't know what it looks like. Probably like all the other little brown birds out there. And I wouldn't be excited by it. Maybe moving up in the rankings requires some measure of novelty as well as showiness. I have in my head a vague notion of the birds that check the right boxes. I think it would only be proper to exclude those species that do not have some connection to the local landscape. I don't know why, but it seems unfair to pit a robin against a bird of paradise, but it's perfectly okay to have a chickadee go up against a pileated woodpecker.

So in addition to some of the ones I've already mentioned, I would also include the following: bald eagle (a great comeback story), red-winged blackbird (for their song as much as their color bars), brown headed cowbird (what a weird look), great horned owl (just badass), great blue heron (for the sound their wings make), scarlet tanager (brilliant color), and the nuthatch. You may want to know why nuthatch makes the cut – the others are all impressive in some immediately identifiable way. Truth is, I don't know. They're just better. Maybe it's because they're jerks. I'd also add the European starling to the list simply for the white edging around their wings, but somehow being an introduced species, despite taking hold and establishing themselves as a part of the local ecology, disqualifies them in my mind. If you're reading this at home and grumbling because I left your favorite bird off the list, too damn bad. Go make your own list, have your own favorites.

There is one glaring omission though, one that hits all those boxes for me – impressive size, bright colors, mysterious vocalizations, not something you see all the time, and good eating to boot. *Meleagris gallopavo silvestris,* the eastern wild turkey. Nobody ever points out a crow or a mourning dove when driving, but I've never been in a car with someone when there were turkeys about that didn't say "Look, turkey!" I think I've just now, while writing this very sentence here, decided. The turkey is the best. I guess Ben Franklin was right.

I unconsciously apply that same "What's better?" question to all kinds of things, even the small to medium sized mammals of the woods. Chipmunks and red squirrels fill the bottom tiers, while the penthouse is reserved for the red fox and river otter. Insects? Ants and mosquitoes to the back of the line, praying mantis and Hercules beetle to the front row please. Fish? Yellow perch and brook trout trounce carp and creek chub every time. I even extend this incessant comparing to amphibians, trees, even fungi. Give me a chicken of the woods mushroom over an artist's conk any day. And it's not about edibility, I don't even like mushrooms.

I suppose extinction is the only way for some of those low scoring species to improve their spot on the leaderboard. People clamor over the disappearance of the passenger pigeon (okay, maybe they're not clamoring, but it's a well-known story and usually gets told with a sense of regret, as though the teller wished for a different outcome), but the passenger pigeon just looks like an even more boring mourning dove, if that's possible. Maybe I would have ranked them higher had I been alive to see the great flocks, but my point stands that extinction has only helped their reputation. The magnificence of the chestnut was surely remarked on when they dominated the eastern forests, but stock prices jumped once they fell to the chestnut blight. If woodchucks succumbed to a deadly virus and there was only one left on the landscape, would I mourn the loss? Would I wish that I had taken more time to appreciate them, spent some time watching the way they raise up on hind legs or scurry away clumsily when startled, or, when he popped his head out of his burrow, would I line up the crosshairs like usual?

I'm not worried about offending any wrens or warblers - they don't, and shouldn't, care what I think. But I am worried that I'm depriving myself in some way by glossing over them in search of something that ranks higher on my list. I like looking at birds, watching them poke around in the grass, flit through the sky, hover in front of a feeder. Each species should be admired for what it is, not what it does for me aesthetically or otherwise. The challenge, for me then, is to allow them – birds, flowers, bugs – to just be, and not expect anything more. To be able to watch a tree swallow cut a graceful arc across the evening horizon and have that be enough.

# "Shall I go to heaven or a-fishing?"

- Thoreau

T old you I'd only bring him up once more. I was initially going to start this essay by saying "My relationship with fishing is a complicated one" because I thought that it sounded cool and mysterious. The problem is of course that it's not complicated at all. Fishing is fun and awesome and anyone who says otherwise is stupid and wrong. The complicating factor is that fishing, in addition to being fun, is also disappointing, boring, and frustrating. And as usual, I blame everyone but myself.

If popular fishing media is to be believed, then largemouth bass are the holy grail of fishing. Any major fishing tournament is all about that bass. Outside of saltwater environs, largemouths dominate the televised sport fishing industry. I've never heard of "Walleye Pro Shops" or seen the "PerchMaster Classic." I'm not knocking bass fishing, I've done – and still do – plenty of it myself. The focus on largemouth was always strange to me, though. They're certainly gorgeous fish, but I've hooked a few big ones and each time it felt more like reeling in a sodden sweatshirt than fighting a game fish. There was just no "oomph" like you get with even a medium sized brown trout. Smallmouth bass are a different story, of course. They're famous for putting up a fight and can present a fun challenge when one is rigged up ultralight for brookies or rainbows.

The weather was going to be clear and calm and finally not twenty degrees, and conditions seemed ripe for a visit to Moraine State Park. The park is centered around a manmade lake that covers about five square miles, and, if the fish commission is to be believed, contains populations of pike, largemouth bass, channel cats, musky, walleye, black crappie, stripers, and bluegill. I've heard this lake referred to as a graveyard and a dead lake, with less than stellar fishing, especially compared to other waterways that are not far off. Doesn't matter, I have fond memories of that lake, going there with my father in our little aluminum boat. We'd motor back into some quiet little cove and sit under the sun and fish. I don't really ever remember catching much, but I must have hooked the occasional fish, otherwise I can't imagine that I'd have continued to go back.

Without a "real" boat now, I was limited to a seventeen-foot Old Town Discovery canoe. A few rods, a couple canoe paddles, a backpack full of tackle, a big long rope tied to a twenty-pound dumbbell for an anchor, and a cooler and I was ready to go. I unloaded at the boat ramp, getting a bit of side eye from people backing in their boat trailers, as if to say "Son, you brought a canoe to a bass boat fight." Whatever, I had bigger issues. Like the fact that even on a calm day the wind has a strange habit of rising out of nowhere as if to say "Where do you think you're going?" I may as well have been dragging a fifty-gallon drum for as much headway as I was making.

Fortunately, this lake is irregularly shaped and offers a number of narrower arms that stretch back into fairly protected coves, turning corners that act as windbreaks. I was soon able to paddle in the approximation of a straight line and reached some calm water. I'd been watching fishing videos online and this water looked like the kind they were always pulling monster bass out of, so I lowered the dumbbell over the side. Twenty pounds may not sound like much, but when you're lowering it over the edge of a canoe things can get a bit unstable. Luckily the worst that happened was that the rope wrapped around my net and then I lost my grip and dropped the weight, and so the net, thus tangled in the rope, went skittering across the bottom of the canoe and over the side. I was able to grab it just in time for the hooks from a crankbait, now also tangled in the writhing rope, to embed themselves in my hand. Breathe in. This is fine. Breathe out. I'm having a great time out here fishing.

There was not a hint of wind nor current now, perfect conditions. I grabbed my baitcasting setup – seven-and-a-half-foot medium heavy rod, twenty-pound braid, Texas-rigged watermelon Senko – and, aiming for a spot just on the weedline in front of me, launched a cast that smacked off the side of the canoe. Everything I read about baitcasters said the problem would be backlash, when the spool keeps spinning after the lure hits the water, resulting in a bird's nest of line that can't be reeled back in. I didn't suffer from backlash simply because I couldn't even time my release correctly to throw a lure farther than a few feet, and always to the left of where I was aiming. The problem was the flexibility of the rod. To this point I'd only ever used very light action rods – think something really bendy, like a fresh cut green willow switch. This rod responded more like a broom handle, and consequently I was waiting too long for my release, sending cast after cast smacking into the water near the hull of the boat.

It's a beautiful day, I'm not discouraged, I can do this. I was tempted to throw the rod as far as I could and watch it cry for help as it sank beneath the surface, that would teach it. But, it wasn't exactly a cheap rod and I'm not a child, I'm a mature adult who can recognize that taking my frustrations out on inanimate objects will solve nothing. I gently laid the rod in the bottom of the canoe. I even managed to not swear out loud until a guy in a kayak rounded the point and immediately caught a bass out of the spot I had been aiming for.

"Hey, look at that! Hoo-wee!"

"Nice fish, man."

"Yeah, they been biting today, got me six in the last two hours."

Game on, basshole.

Switching to a more familiar combo – flexible rod instead of heavy action, swapping the baitcaster for a spinning reel, and adding a secret weapon, the unbeatable live nightcrawler, I sent a long zinging cast to my spot. Perfect placement. Not a gust of wind, not a ripple of current, and yet I soon, and I mean like within seconds, find myself pointed in the opposite direction. My line extending back over my shoulder to the spot which is now behind me. I lower the rod tip and turn to face the back of the canoe in order to better work the bait through the weed edges. A tug, a bite! I set the hook on what turns out to be a stick. It's not even like a fish shaped stick or anything. Just a twig. I hate not catching fish. I hate not catching fish in front of other people even more.

The moment, and the spot, ruined for me, I pull up my anchor and set off. At least, I try to pull up my anchor. The lake bottom is apparently made of glue, and the canoe lurches suddenly to the side as I try to retrieve my weight. The spare paddle, extra rods, fishing net, and cooler all slide to the side as the right gunwale drops dangerously close to the water, further unbalancing things. The open container of nightcrawlers is about to topple but I can't reach over to stop it because that would mean removing one hand from the rope and throwing the balance off even more. I watch helplessly as they spill out across the bottom of the canoe. With what I can only imagine would be a giant sucking sound were it not under twenty feet of water, the dumbbell begins to give. I take the line in hand over hand until I can grasp the weight and toss it behind my seat in the stern of the canoe. Right directly onto the jacket I had placed back there earlier. There's black mud and the stench of decay, and I swear to god if that guy catches another fish I'm going to use him for an anchor.

I paddle for fifteen minutes or so, chalking up the last spot to a loss. I ease into a narrow cove that looks like bass heaven. Drop offs and structure everywhere. Downed trees thrust out from the shoreline, providing perfect hiding spots and cover for baitfish, and perfect places for big old wary bass to ambush them. I switch to a topwater frog because I once heard someone say the words "topwater frog" while they were fishing for bass. This thing is so incredibly realistic in the water. I'm impressed. If I ate frogs I'd be all over it. The bass, however, are not. See, the problem with fishing is that certain things only work at certain times, and apparently topwater fishing in the middle of the afternoon is something that's going to get you skunked at best, and laughed off the lake at worst. It doesn't even matter now, because no sooner had I reeled in my incredibly lifelike frog than the sound of shouting and chainsaws broke the tranquility. I now noticed the rental cabins dotting the shoreline, and though they weren't being used at the moment, the area was being prepared for their eventual occupation. A crew of four guys began dropping trees all around me, seemingly oblivious to my presence. They were clearing the paths and beach areas around the cabins, and it just so happened that all the trees were dropping right into the channel I was sitting in. I wasn't in any danger of being hit by anything, of course, but I couldn't help but feel like maybe this wasn't the spot for a peaceful afternoon float. I paddled on.

At some point, bad luck and misfortune begin to amuse me. Kind of like a "What could possibly go wrong next?" feeling, but in a way where I've given up on being mad about it. I look at it like I'm now the winner of the bad luck Olympics, anything more is only padding my stats. Rationalizations in hand, I pulled my canoe up onto one of the few shallow grades on the shoreline. Much of the lakeshore is quite steep, with few places that are walkable and conducive to shore fishing, which is why I brought the canoe in the first place. But this spot was speaking to me like one of the Sirens. "Pull up, take a break" it said. There was a tree that had fallen into the water, sticking out maybe forty feet. This one was not cut deliberately. The bank had given way and the dirt packed root ball provided enough shade to the point where I could sit in the stern of the boat, facing out towards the submerged treetop, and not be subjected to the direct sunlight. The lake bottom was shallow and sloped gradually downward, with what appeared to be a drop off about ten feet out. I tried topwaters. I tried spinners. I tried a jig, a creature bait, a stickbait. I had a four-and-a-half-foot ultralight rod with a micro spinning reel and four-pound mono. I added the tiniest barbed hook, threaded on a half-inch piece of redworm, then I put on the smallest bobber that I had (I might make some enemies here, but. . . Strike indicator? That's a bobber, man, come off it.)

For the next hour I sat there and caught one four-inch bluegill after another. Every time that bobber would pop below the surface I'd get a giddy little rush. The rod tip would bend double the way a regular pole would under the pressure of a two-pound smallmouth. And I'd wager that, ounce for ounce, those bluegill fight harder than any largemouth bass. It might sound like I'm trying to whitewash a bad fishing trip or trick myself into thinking I had a good time. I don't need to trick myself into it, it was a blast. I'll bet I was having more fun than the guy on the boat a hundred yards away trying to nab that five-pound largemouth that didn't exist.

# Rock and Roll Ain't Noise Pollution

I f I could uninvent one thing, I'd uninvent the guy who only let me
pick one thing to uninvent. Because man have I got some gripes.
I know a guy who is locally famous for his tremendous rants
against whatever he finds ridiculous that day; walnuts on salad, people
with multiple middle names, classic rock fans that don't like Warren
Zevon, bike lanes. They're brief, furious and ultimately humorous tirades
that distract us from the kinds of things people want to be distracted
from. Like an M-80 in a toilet, there's a flash and a bang and it's all over
in a few seconds. I tend to be less M-80 and more underground coal fire.
My hatred for things burns slow and long and can't be extinguished with
any but the most drastic measures. You ever hear of Centralia,
Pennsylvania? That's the kind of burn I'm talking about when it comes
to noise pollution. (For the uninitiated, a coal seam beneath Centralia has
basically been on fire since 1962.)

By noise pollution I don't just mean the sounds of city traffic, freight trains, or babies laughing. No, there are far worse culprits out there. The top spot is currently held by what seems to have become the most ubiquitous tool of suburban living. You may be forgiven for thinking that I'm talking about the gas-powered lawnmower. After all, nearly every house has one, and as soon as the sun comes out so, too, does the incessant whirring of blades of all types and sizes – mulching blades, cutting blades, whatever blade it is that my neighbor has that goes "uhnuhnuhnCLANGuhnuhnSKREEcoughwheeze", you know the one. No, lawnmowers don't make the cut, and for a simple yet strange reason. I can get over the sound of a mower simply because it's ignorable. Growing up, my parents had a cuckoo clock. You probably remember the one, with the big ass pinecones for weights and the weird birdhouse thing from which a vaguely bird shaped creature would emerge to make a sound that no bird ever made. And not just once, but one hundred and eighty times. Every. Single. Day. Cuckoo clocks, at least the one I grew up with, make more noise than just the chiming every half hour, though. There was also an oak leaf shaped pendulum that would swing back and forth, once every second. It would make a ticking sound each time. That's eighty-six thousand four hundred little ticks per day. Together that makes eighty-six thousand five hundred and eighty little noises made over the course of every twenty-four-hour period.

The thing is, you hardly ever noticed it. You had to really be paying attention to even realize that there was any noise at all. The ticking of the pendulum was most noticeable when you first walked in the door after having been gone a bit. It's as though the human ear experiences sound fatigue after a certain period of time, like the brain hears it, recognizes that it's not important, and then blocks it out. I think most human senses work in a similar fashion. After all, our senses were honed in a world where distinguishing between things that were a part of our environment, and things that were a part of our environment that wanted to kill and eat us, meant the difference between surviving or becoming another one of Darwin's bitches. You ever walk in to friend's house and immediately think "How the hell can you live in a place that smells this strongly of cat piss?" and then after a couple hours and a few beers you completely forget about it, but then when you get out to your car to drive home you realize you forgot your keys and so you walk back in and are olfactorily offended all over again? Okay, so that's why lawnmowers don't bother me. They are initially loud but quickly fade to ignorable background noise. So, no, if you guessed lawnmower you were wrong. But you were close.

The real offender here is, of course, the leaf blower. And, no, I'm not a looney or a crotchety old geezer. I hope to be one someday, but no, leaf blowers really are the devil's noisemaker. Think about it. The World Health Organization recommends a general daytime outdoor noise level of 55 Decibels. At the source, a leaf blower measures between 95 and 110 Decibels. But of course, the operator isn't bothered by it. They're probably wearing ear protection, but, more importantly, they're the one in control of the noise. They know when to expect an increase in volume and are in control of how long that noise will last. A neighbor or pedestrian? Not so much. At a distance of fifty feet, which could span three houses in my neighborhood, the typical level is 65 to 80 Decibels. The problem with the leaf blower is its intermittent nature. It's not a sustained and ignorable sound, and so each new blast is that much more noticeable.

My other problem with leaf blowers is that they offend me on a more basic level, one that I'm not proud of, but that I can't simply deny or turn off. Maybe it's part of my dream of becoming a crotchety old man who can yell at kids for being on his lawn, but I just want to know, "What's wrong with a rake?!?" If you want to move a bunch of leaves, there's no tool better than a rake. It's an enjoyable activity, raking leaves. Maybe not when you're nine and your dad is yelling at you and you accidentally grabbed a handful of dog poop when you were putting the leaves into the big garbage bag, but as father with kids you can yell at? It's almost as good as football. Leaf blowers are the lazy man's way of dealing with a problem that we really all just collectively decided should be a thing. Imagine if we as a society decided that leaves were a great lawn decoration – more leaves meant higher status or something. But no, we just have to make more pointless work for ourselves.

The other problem I have with leaf blowers is that, more than any other value conscious group of people I've ever encountered, including "extreme couponers", leaf blower people want to make sure they get their money's worth. That means blowing leaves every day, sometimes even every hour – you can't let that maple leaf lay on the grass for a second, gotta get rid of it. But what about all the other seasons? Oh boy. Let. Me. Tell. You.

Early winter – use it to blow the small accumulation of snow off your sidewalk and car.

Mid-winter – blow snow off your front steps, sidewalk, and car.

Late winter – blow snow off your roof

Early spring – blow pollen from pine trees off your car

Late spring – blow grass clippings off your sidewalk

Early summer – blow birds' nests off your porch, leaves out of your gutter, and frisbees off your roof.

Late summer – blow dry your car after washing it (I wish I was making that one up.)

It's incessant, annoying, and unnecessary. If you live in a suburban area, go out on your porch on a nice day and see if you can count how many different leaf blowers you can hear. It should be illegal. If someone ever invents a quieter leaf blower, buy stock, because I can't imagine I'm the only person who feels this way.

While a leaf blower may interrupt my suburban porch swing reverie, there's another noise pollution culprit out there that may be an even more egregious offender. I'm probably in the minority here, especially among the outdoor enthusiast crowd, but I would say that ATVs rank up there in terms of things that piss me off because of the noise they make. Quads, four wheelers, offroaders, whatever you call them, they're obnoxious and have no place in the outdoors. You want to race around all fast and loud? Go drive on any highway (hint - you can go way faster in your Hyundai that you ever could on an ATV.) Much like a leaf blower, an ATV may provide the user with ease and convenience, but it comes at the cost of the peace and serenity of everyone else within a half mile radius. I can't count the number of hunting trips that I've had busted because someone was too lazy to haul their fat ass on foot through the woods actually looking at things instead of tear-assing around. I really don't think that I'm alone in thinking that part of the enjoyment of hunting is in seeing nature's creatures walking around naturally doing natural stuff. You're not going to see any of that from your Polaris or Honda or TrailCrusherMegaBossXtreme or whatever.

Admittedly, my issues with four-wheelers run a little deeper than simply noise. Sometime in the last couple years some jagoff decided it would be a good idea to drive in to the camp property from the adjacent dirt road, only they apparently wanted to do it in a very particular location. Then, once a path was established, others decided it looked like a good place to drive and throw beer cans, and it was soon a two-track path cutting through one of my most productive hunting locations. Imagine, it's your last archery hunt of the 2019 season. You've been chasing a wide 8-point all year and, based on everything you've learned from relentlessly studying this buck, he should be rolling through sometime this evening. Everything is perfect, conditions couldn't be better. Then you hear it, the BLAAAAAT of a quad rolling in from the road. You get pissed, climb down, chase down the offender – "Oh sorry, I didn't know anyone was hunting here, I'm just looking for does." – Yeah, like you'll see any animals that way, carting your fat ass around in that thing. It even had a radio and a heater. Dude, if you want to be in a house, stay home.

The ATV track from the road has been blocked by several large trees my father and I cut down and pushed into place using the tractor (another loud and obnoxious machine, I agree, but one whose utilitarian nature makes it acceptable. At least to me. You may feel different when stuck behind one on a country highway.) I guess we'll find out of the four-wheeled offenders are simply inconsiderate (that is, they decide maybe they should find different trails to access), or if they're actually complete assholes (as in, they just decide to drive around the new barrier.) It kind of makes me wish that land mines were legal.

# Hillbilly Rites of Passage

I consider myself pretty progressive when it comes to issues surrounding gender differences. I wouldn't avoid voting for someone because they were a woman, I wouldn't distrust a nurse simply because they were a man, and I wouldn't assume that any gender would be more qualified to hold any particular occupation, unless it was something like professional testicle model or breast feeding advice columnist. Then maybe I'd have to insist. After all, I'm a public-school teacher, an occupation that is 76% female. Narrowing things down to "public high school teacher" still leaves women with the edge at 64%. And damned if I don't think I still do a pretty good job. All right, an okay job. You know what, forget that example. Of course, this is all just a clever setup to get the reader wondering "what kind of sexist thing is he going to say now?" Because that's what we do, isn't it?

"I'm not racist but…",

"Now, don't think me homophobic. . ."

"I'm not saying that *all* vegetarians are granola munching devil worshippers,"

But there are differences. And truthfully, I don't know anybody, from "My name's Bubba but people call me Fat Bubba" to "It's spelled F-I-O-N-A but it's pronounced like the way a rainbow smells" that would dispute that. (Have I mentioned that I'm also great at building straw men?)

So one of the more uniquely male activities I participate in is what's become known as "hillbilly weekend." Uniquely male because it's just a bunch of dudes from work, hillbilly because we're north of I-80, the clear Pennsylvania dividing line between owns-a collared-shirt and occasionally-eats-possum, and weekend because most of us simply exist Monday to Friday living for that precious twenty-eight and a half percent of the time we're not toiling away in the salt mines that are our full time jobs.

There's an awful lot of swearing, plenty of crude humor, ungodly quantities of alcohol, fire, grilled meat, classic rock, and stupidity. Does that mean that a bunch of women couldn't get together and drink themselves stupid while swearing and being crude? Please, that's called a bachelorette party. Really the only thing that makes it "guy stuff" is that we all decided to leave our significant others at home. Hell, my wife is a routine witness to me drinking too much, saying something crass, gorging myself on meat and then passing out in the yard. The difference is, she doesn't seem to want to participate. Probably because we have kids and she's a responsible mother and not a human dumpster fire.

So what is it about a "guy's weekend" that's such a universal draw? I think it has a little bit to do with there being a level of competition, be it the annual whiffle ball contest (old guys vs young guys), the fishing (because you're always competing when you're fishing), or even "whose man enough to make breakfast without puking" (hint: not me.) But these competitions don't reward winners or punish losers, they merely serve as a means for us to test ourselves in ways that often seem discouraged in the real world. How many people have learned important things about themselves after hearing someone else say the words "I dare you to . . ." Half my awesome story repertoire only exists because someone else challenged me to do something dumb. Because, at least in my head, "do something dumb" translates to "push yourself and test your abilities." To be clear, we weren't daring each other to play Russian Roulette or drink bleach, more along the lines of

"I bet you won't kayak over that waterfall."

"I bet you don't have the balls to talk to that girl over there."

"I bet you can't eat a dozen donuts in less than three minutes."

Okay, there may have been some measure of irresponsible bravado that might have ended badly, but it was never anything overly dangerous. Just things that still required a level of discomfort, physical or otherwise.

Historically, other cultures have always had "coming of age" rituals. These were typically directed towards the boys within the tribe. Challenges. Obstacles. Things that a boy could do to not only prove his worth and bravery, but also to ceremonially mark the transition from boyhood to manhood. Were we to have such rituals now I think they would be pretty well frowned upon, and deservedly so. Who sends a thirteen-year-old out into the woods alone for a week and tasks him with bringing back the claws or teeth or talons of the area's most dangerous predator? And yet, this "test yourself" mentality is what builds confidence and self-assuredness. You don't have confidence in your ability to do something until you've done it. I think young men today often suffer from a crisis of confidence, having so few outlets with which to test themselves. The closest thing I can think of is organized sports, and if you want to get me all wound up and going off about something, this is a good starting point. Do the thing first, the confidence comes later, and that makes each subsequent endeavor a little less scary.

Hillbilly weekend has fulfilled that role for me. Throw in the primal attraction of sitting around a fire, and we may as well be 500,000-year-old *Homo heidelbergensis* comparing various hunting successes or testing our spear throwing prowess. I'm too lazy to research it, but I suspect the Olympics had similar beginnings. So much of modern life is spent trying to eliminate the challenges faced by early humans. Don't get me wrong, I'm glad I don't have to compete with saber toothed cats during my morning commute, but what has become of that hard-wired evolutionary vigilance? What other avenues does it have for expression or alleviation? I suspect (without any research or proof, of course) that the rise of things like anxiety disorders are a direct result of our removal from nature and the constant pressures we faced as a species while evolving. You can't be worried about whether or not your boss's partner thought you were awkward at the Christmas party if you're too busy looking for food and keeping an eye out for bears. As a species we're very young, no more than 200,000 years old. That may seem like a long time, but in evolutionary terms it's nothing, a mere fraction of a second of the great geologic clock. Developed nations struggle with obesity because, despite it being unhealthy and shortening lifespans, the craving for foods high in fat and calories is an evolutionarily hardwired holdover from a time where it contributed significantly to survival. Shedding our ancestral habits is not an easy task. The need for pushing boundaries and testing limits is an equally established part of our evolutionary history. New, more productive hunting grounds were the province of those with the desire or compulsion to answer the question "What's over there?" Risk takers.

Hillbilly weekend also approximates a modern form of tribalism. People want to belong, they want to have a group. Otherwise you end up with school shooters and scientology. Hanging out for the weekend in the woods with a bunch of dudes (hold your jokes until the end of the program) provides that sense of belonging. It's funny, the original getaway was, and still is, referred to simply as "camp." I'd heard stories for years about camp shenanigans. Inside jokes, references, that kind of thing. Admittedly I'm a little bit (a lot) prickly and take some warming up to, so when I finally got the invite to "camp" I was excited. Excited to attend, to be a part of something that was talked about and referenced throughout the year, but mostly excited to have a "tribe" again. My first year of camp attendance may have made me a part of that tribe, but I really can't remember. Something about falling in a garbage can and a bunch of unexplained bruises are the only memories I have. I was just happy to be there.

We're all considerably older now. Bedtime comes a bit earlier, hangovers last a bit longer. Venues changed. We've replaced drunken whiffle ball with leisurely canoe floats. There's still plenty of fire and cursing, but we're fortunate to have come to a point in our lives where we're comfortable with ourselves. We know our abilities and limitations, and that makes for a group of guys that are just content to hang out, maybe sorting out our pecking order over a game of cornhole.

# Year in Review

There must exist some sort of rule that if you write a book about nature, specifically a particular location that is "in nature", you have to include a section that details the environmental changes that take place over the course of a year. Maybe it's done by the changes in season, maybe it's month to month, some rely on summaries from the author's personal journals. In any case, you've got to have a year in review.

It might sound like I'm not a fan of this construction, but quite the contrary. I absolutely love reading about the seasonal changes that occur. The shift in animal sightings, particularly birds, is especially interesting. I like to read about the ways that the author connects with the land during its various stages. There's also a satisfaction that comes with reading a full circle story – January to January or what have you, like a cliché country song. There's comfort in reading about so many changes, seemingly so drastic, yet ultimately ending right back where you started. It's reassuring in a way. In that same spirit, I figured I would present to you, dear reader, a one-year snapshot of life at the cabin.

January, 2019

Okay, so I didn't go to the property at all in January. I imagine it was probably pretty cold.

February 23rd, 2019

"It's cold here. Damn is it cold."

March 30th, 2019

"The rain has picked up; it's supposed to snow tonight. Pretty chilly."

(It gets better, I promise. At least I hope so, because going back and reading these entries is making me wonder why I romanticize this place so much.)

April 18th – April 21st, 2019

"More rain today. Smoked some ribs, they came out okay. Ticks are everywhere. Tried turkey hunting with OJ in the morning but it was raining and cold so we only lasted an hour."

May 25th, 2019

"Just me and the dogs and Lou and Badger. Arr. at 12:30. Hot and sunny. Planted potatoes carrots peppers and beans, placed 3 trail cams. Then it rained. And rained. And rained. Played cribbage until 12:00 AM, dogs got me up at 5:30. Planted chestnut trees Sunday morning and came home."

June 13th – 15th, 2019

"Larry's dogs killed some skunks and he came by with a small one by the tail, apparently they can't spray if you hold the tail. Saw turkey come off the roost by the dead ash tree – Davey scared her up - and a velvet buck. Corn and beans are up, some potatoes too. No peppers yet. Broke a belt on the tractor."

July 2nd – July 4th, 2019

"It rained and rained. Tried to cut grass Thursday morning but the belt slipped and then the tractor wouldn't start and I messed with it for 2 hrs and got Larry to help fix it. Packed up and came home to a leaky water heater and an unfinished bathroom."

August 8th – August 10th, 2019

"Just me and the dogs today, and Lou and Badger. Thunderstorms, cutting grass, tilling fields, running the drags and the rollers and some prescribed fire. Found a snake giving live birth in the gas well food plot. Pretty cool, think maybe ringneck? Got the tractor stuck on the side hill. Beat Lou in cribbage. Ate steak."

September 6th, 2019

"Just for the day. Cut grass, got rained on. Dug tons of red potatoes and carrots, also some beans and onions. Set up two blinds. 1 hr traffic jam on the way home."

October 18th – October 20th, 2019

"Fell asleep on the porch in the sun. Gathered walnuts. Evening hunt in the treehouse with Molly. Nothing from 4:30 – 6:30, then a seven-point emerged. She had to wait forever for him to turn but she stuck it out and got her buck."

November 15th, 2019

"Got up at 6:30. 33 degrees downstairs and 17 degrees outside. Sat the gravel pit tree stand from 7:00 to 8:30. Big 8 point showed up off the racetrack later, no possible shot though. Packed it in early and left at 4:00."

December 14th, 2019

"Time to make sausage. 3 lbs pork fat, 9 lbs venison, 4 Tbsps fennel, 3 Tbsps coarse salt, red pepper flakes, loads of black pepper, 3 Tbsps minced garlic. 2.5 lbs loose, rest in links. God do these casings smell terrible."

So there you have it, life at the cabin oscillates between seasons of "cold," "colder," "rainy," and "tractor problems."

The changes that take place there are always welcome and a little surprising. I know the apple trees will break out in an explosion of blossoms every year, yet arriving there after having been gone for two weeks and seeing the previously bare branches blushed out in sprays of pink and white always gives me jolt. Spotting that first buck to have put on velvet, enduring that first night of the year when it gets cold enough to build a fire. Waking to the first snow of the year muting every color, movement, and sound. The streams and hills don't change, the forest is still the same, but it's also not. It's dynamic, remade again and again, the seasonal changes reflected in the short term with the passing of each day.

# How to Cook a Dead Animal

In the interest of self-preservation, I offer up the disclaimer that there's a good chance my memory is inaccurate, but if I was held to it, I'd say that my mother had a pretty steady rotation of dishes she would serve up for dinner each day. That, in itself, is neither controversial nor unusual, I imagine it's the same way in households across the world. I'll also start by saying my mother made some of the best pork chops I've ever eaten. Now, Mom, if you're reading this, that's the end of the story. As far as you're concerned the rest of this is about boring stuff you have no interest in, like maybe global grain exports or the chemical composition of the Saturnine atmosphere.

Okay, so included in her repertoire were a couple of dishes that I just can't believe were things that real humans actually ate. Like stuff served up for people. On a regular basis. They were edible, to be sure, but just . . . I don't know. The first was mince. Let me explain, my mother is half-Scottish, half-French. You'd think that would give me the opportunity to grow up on coq au vin, éclairs, and crêpes. I think mince must be from the Scottish side. After all, their national dish is haggis or something. Anyways, mince consisted of ground beef fried in a cast iron skillet. I think maybe it had carrots cut up in it, and maybe some salt. That was it, that was dinner. If it was extra fancy you'd layer it with mashed potatoes and peas and call it shepherd's pie.

"Ooh, we're having pie for dinner?!"

Yeah, no, that was a damn lie.

I think the major contributing factor was that my parents, in addition to thinking you could make something with meat and potatoes and call it a pie, didn't seem to believe in seasonings. After I was married my wife and I were at my folks' house and we were going to make dinner. Something innocuous like lasagna, I believe.

"Where's your garlic powder?"

"I don't think we have any."

"How do you not have garlic powder, it's like the single most used seasoning after salt and pepper!"

"Look in the lazy Susan."

So I looked. You know what I found? Some black peppercorns, oregano, and mustard seed. All in glass bottles with faded labels and plastic tops of that special green color only found in 1960's kitchens.

"How the hell old are these seasonings?"

"Oh, I think we got those as a wedding gift."

They were married in something like 1972. This conversation took place in 2008.

There was another dish that occurred with more frequency than I enjoyed, and that was boiled potatoes with cauliflower and cheese sauce. I think maybe you boiled the potatoes and cauliflower until they were indistinguishable from each other, and then mixed it all together with some cheese that was melted in butter with some added flour? I think? I really have tried to block it out. The point is, I was, with good reason, not an adventurous eater. Chicken and macaroni and PB&J were more my speed. I don't think I had a taco until I was a junior in high school.

Predictably, wild game was not a common occurrence at the table growing up. I know we fished, first day of trout every year, but I don't think we ever kept any. I know we had to have had venison on at least one occasion, because I distinctly remember not liking it. I think I was in my mid-thirties when I made the dedicated decision to get a deer processed and try to turn it into dinner. This was a big step.

That first one gave me some trouble. Having never cooked it before, I sought out advice.

"Grind it all up into chili and use lots of garlic."

"It dries out fast so you should soak it in A-1 for a couple days."

"Cook it real low, like a hundred degrees, for eight hours."

Yes, venison is lean. Yes, it can contain off flavors. Off flavors have been attributed to blood in the meat, fat on the meat, the animal being stressed when it died, what the deer was eating, contamination from the tarsal gland, improper gutting, not aging it enough, aging it too much; it's all enough to scare any novice away, or at least make them think that it's not worth it when the grocery store has a 2 for 1 sale on top round. If you find yourself reluctant to wade the wild game waters, here's an easy 3 step guide for failsafe cooking.

1. Trim your meat. Cut off anything that doesn't look like rich, dark red meat. All sinew, fat, and silverskin. I find that these connective tissues, above all else, are the reason people are turned off of venison every year. As you gain experience it will be easier to know what you can

let slide – meat for a roast and meat for the grind pile can be treated differently. But this is a simple guide, so – Trim. Your. Meat.

2. Season with salt and pepper. Load up on that stuff. Make like you're creating a dry rub out of it. Add other things if you want, thyme, rosemary, garlic. Just don't go overboard.

3. Sear the outside, then cook in an oven until it reaches 125°. Or, get all fancy and do a reverse sear, which brings it up to temperature first and then sears it after. Whatever.

This is where I'm supposed to say "Done right, it's indistinguishable from beef." Except that's not true, and it shouldn't be. If you want beef, eat beef. Stop approaching venison as if it's some inedible product that needs to be transformed into something familiar in order to taste good. That's like when vegetarian food companies try to make plant-based imitations of meat. If you want plants, eat plants! There's nothing wrong with that. You don't see the pork industry out there being all "BrusselSnouts! The pork based brussel sprout substitute. Get yours today!" That's because pork tastes good as pork. And venison tastes good as venison.

It can be hard to get past the mental block many of us have when it comes to food. I was at an authentic Mexican restaurant many years ago, and, not knowing what would be good, I opted for what I thought would be the safest choice – the soup. The soup of the day was menudo, which I of course had never heard of before. The flavor was good, if a bit spicy. Lots of chunks of vegetables, and some meat. It had a snappy texture to it that was unfamiliar but not unpleasant. While still in the restaurant, after I had finished it all, a "friend" I was with clued me in on what makes menudo, menudo. I, and this is embarrassing to relive, began to gag. It turns out I can't stomach stomach.

I recently tried to expand my family's palate beyond venison burgers and roasts, with a pan-fried heart recipe. My younger two children enjoyed it, said it tasted good, and agreed we should save the hearts from all our future deer to be done in this fashion. My oldest agreed that the taste was good, but was unlikely to want to have it again. I tried it. That same snappy texture that I recall from menudo was not what I was expecting. Like my oldest, I thought the flavor was fine, but that mental block - "You're eating heart, you're eating heart, you're eating heart" like its own rhythmic beat – was, embarrassingly still there. My wife avoided the experience all together.

Next season, I'm going to take the advice of my two younger children. We're going to keep those hearts, we're going to cook them, and we're going to enjoy them. My wife has even agreed to potentially consider thinking about maybe attempting to try it too. I wonder if she knows what rocky mountain oysters are.

# A Love Letter to My Wife
## (Wanna Go Campin'?)

How do couples that have never gone camping together know that they're ready to get married? This isn't a joke, I'm actually looking for an answer. Okay, so maybe it's not the only yardstick that can be used to gauge the potential for marital success, but it's a pretty darn good one. Way better than premarital counseling, in my opinion. It's easy for a couple to sound like they're in agreement when everyone is well fed and well rested and not suffering from sunburns or poison ivy. And if you're anything like me, premarital counseling (something that was required by whomever it was that performed our ceremony) is viewed as a test you have to pass. Is this pastor/minister/whatever going to refuse to do it if I give the wrong answer? So what do you do? You cheat.

"Okay honey, if she asks, we want two children. And we want to wait until we're financially stable but we also understand that unexpected things happen. And my favorite color is green."

I mean, I get it. If a couple comes in for counseling and suddenly finds out that they want completely different things and that the only thing they have in common is that they're horny and lonely, then yeah, maybe they can be talked out of a dumb decision. But for regular folk? A camping trip is the best counselor you could ask for.

My wife is more housecat than mountain lion. She could maybe kill me the way a mountain lion would if she found out I was comparing her infinite beauty, grace, and intelligence to a bunch of mangy felines, but our premarital counselor never said not to, so . . . What I mean is that she's not really the outdoors type. Which makes the fact that we've been married 18 years an accomplishment worth bragging about. And it probably wouldn't have happened had we not taken a camping trip together first. (Bet you regret that trip now, don't you dear?)

I'm not sure of the outdoors pedigree of every potential reader of this potential book, so I feel I need to explain "camping trip." I don't mean camping like pitching a tent at a K.O.A. for a day, or spending a night in the local state park. It was two days of driving cross-country non-stop followed by a week of backpacking in the Bridger Teton National Forest. It's a trip of a lifetime, everything you could possibly hope for in an outdoor adventure, and maybe not the best way to introduce someone to camping for the first time. I'm fairly sure that, up until this point, my (future) wife had never done any of the following:

Gone to the bathroom in the woods.

Bathed in a stream.

Had sunburn under her fingernails.

Hiked seventy miles.

Slept in a tent.

Eaten something cooked in the coals of a fire.

Seen a bear.

Run away from a bear.

Slept out under the stars.

Awoke to a grasshopper on her face.

Hunkered under a pine tree for shelter during a July hailstorm.

Forded a swift river pantsless, boots slung around her neck.

And a great many other things. To be fair, I hadn't ever done a couple of those things either, but in my case they were things I was actively looking forward to. If you and your potential partner come out the other end of a trip like that and you're both still on speaking terms, or at least still using hand gestures, then that's a good sign.

There's nothing quite like the "getting to know you" phase of a relationship. Everything is perfect, you're never in a bad mood around the other person, you always have clean underwear on . . . DO NOT rely on the camping trip test during this period of a relationship. It won't work. First of all, you'll be too busy engaging in "activities" to learn anything substantial about the other person except for maybe strange birthmarks or fetishes. More importantly though, you're still in the stage of the relationship where you won't fart in front of the other person or tell them if they have something stuck in their teeth. You're trying to impress, and so are they, so gripes go ungriped, disgusts go undiscussed, and there will just be a nervous sort of unease that's buried under the aforementioned activities. It's an intoxicating stage of any relationship, and it's little wonder that people can jump from one to the next chasing that novel high. Rookies.

No, the camping trip test is for those relationships that have developed beyond those initial stages. The ones where you get to see her without makeup and she learns that your apartment is usually messy and that you sometimes forget to flush the toilet. You've had a few fights, always about stupid things, but you make up afterwards and that's always fun. We were at that stage, and had you asked me then I would have said that yeah, we were ready to get married. In the end I was proven right, but I still didn't really know. The problem was that I didn't *know* that I didn't know.

A week is not a long time unless you're talking about a week being sober or a week stuck listening to your vacationing neighbor's smoke detector. In terms of relationships, it's a drop in the bucket. But when that week tests the limits of a person's endurance, tolerance for discomfort, and even a few flat-out scary moments, it's more informative and educational than a year of living together under ideal conditions. The thing about big long camping trips is that they're new and exciting while you're doing them, but they kind of suck. Hiking ten or fifteen miles sounds great until you're only on mile two and your shoulder is starting to hurt and you're thirsty and kinda tired. And then you just begin dreading the rest of the hike. About that time there's this thing I think of as the zombie wall – either you give up, or you trudge onward, zombie-like, watching the three feet of ground in front of your boots. You vaguely take in some scenic views, you force yourself to swallow some dry granola to keep you going, and you just kind of zone out. It's the same way with paddling a canoe across miles and miles of lakes. Head down, move limb, move other limb, repeat. Why do it then? Because you know you'll have the opportunity to enjoy looking back on the trip. Some of my favorite wilderness trips were miserable in the moment, but the knowledge that the memories would develop flavor over time was enough incentive to continue. And that, in itself, made everything easier.

I was familiar with this phenomenon, she was not. So far, she was only inducted into the misery faction of the club. So when I felt myself getting ready to complain, I looked to see how she was coping. Though probably being more uncomfortable than me, there she was, toughing it out. Stoic, burdened, but not defeated, not relenting. She was solid. What if she was just suffering in silence to impress me? Call me impressed. Imagine how she'd do in a situation that really called for perseverance, guts, or grit.

I don't remember exactly, but we might have even joked about being ready for marriage on the drive home. I know our first stop, before anything else, was at a Rite-Aid 1-hour photo desk. I think I spent $75 dollars getting a bunch of rolls of film developed – you see kids, cameras used to have this thing called "film" and . . .

We spent a day putting the pictures in an album together, writing little captions about what happened or where we were. Photo albums, at least physical ones, have kind of gone out of style. Everything is smartphone camera rolls these days, but we do still have two physical books full of pictures. One is our wedding album, and the other is from that week spent camping in Wyoming.

# Trail Mix

W hile camped in a meadow in Wyoming, I once spent three drizzle-dampened hours prostrate next to a small stream. I was watching the progress of a spider, I don't know what kind, as it built a web between two long blades of grass about eight inches apart. The web was mostly complete when I showed up, but the spider was still hard at work. Watching any individual minute would have yielded little in the way of understanding how a web is made — it would be like trying to deduce the changing of the seasons by taking one temperature recording every day for three months. An incomplete understanding, for sure. But with patience came the realization that there was a distinct system in place. A mathematical, logical, geometric system that was no doubt maximized for efficiency and strength. As the minutes passed, it became clear that there was a particular strand of filament that the spider was using as a main thoroughfare, always returning to it in order to cross the nearly completed web. Some kind of path. I don't know if that particular strand was thicker than the others or if it was free from the sticky excretions that made prey entanglement more likely, or how the spider "knew" that it should use that one filament to get repeatedly from A to B. I don't know if any amount of watching would have made that clear.

Curiously, as though a time-lapse film had begun playing, I began to notice other tiny insects about. The most obvious was what I at first thought to be a single, possibly disoriented, ant. He'd be here, then over there, then back here again. Of course, taking my eyes off the spider, I soon came to find that it was a file of ants all utilizing the same trail. They were moving in an upstream direction. None of the them appeared to be carrying anything the way you would expect a file of army ants to be doing after a successful raid. These were small black ants without any noticeable jaws. I don't know if they were migrating or searching for food, but they came steadily yet widely spaced, mostly single file, for the next hour. I was really hoping to see one blunder into the spider's web so I could watch the aftermath, but they did not deviate from their line. So of course, I grabbed one and dropped him onto the web to speed up the process.

When the ant first contacted the web, the spider froze, nearly at the outer edge. The ant bounced off one thread and into another, his little ant legs flailing. He worked free of that strand, dropping closer to the ground, the spider still unmoving. This was like the world's worst spider because damned if that ant didn't hit like eight different filaments on his way down, not getting tangled, snared, or glued by a single one. I suspect the spider was expecting this, because it never moved from its perch on the outer rim of the web. The ant dropped to the ground, ran around in circles for a bit, and I eventually lost it in the grass. The spider retraced its old steps along the transportation filament towards the center of the web — I'd like to think it was checking to make sure everything was still up to code — and then retreated back to the edge.

"Screw this", I thought. I waited not more than half a minute and then secured another ant. Same result. I didn't bother to try a third time. The spider had a trail it would follow in order to best construct the web, and the ants had their own trail leading them to wherever it was they were headed. Apparently there was also a game trail nearby, because my small-scale reverie was interrupted by my hiking partner calling for my attention. A cow moose and her calf had emerged in the meadow, and not at a distance that I was comfortable with. I backtracked a ways to sit with my friend and watch as the moose grazed in the meadow. It's hard to describe the size of an adult moose without sounding like you've been searching a thesaurus looking for the most superlative adjectives you can find, so I'll just say that they're big. You'd think something of that size would leave much clearer indications of its comings and goings, but when I walked over to where the moose had disappeared back into the woods, there was little to mark their passage. At least, little to my eye.

Trails are hidden all over, often in forms that are not readily apparent to us. There's an area of woods where I frequently hunt that I know, at least in my mind, like the back of my hand. I was working my way up to a tree stand by a familiar path in the aftermath of a light morning snow. The snow had filtered through the trees and had begun to collect on the ground in high spots and hollows. I eventually became aware of a trail I had not seen before. Its presence was only highlighted when the falling snow collected more evenly on the path when compared to the edges. It was clearly a deer path, curving slightly as it sidehilled its way into a stand of hemlock. No doubt it had been there for years, and used for years, but this was the first I had seen of it. Looking through the woods, I began to see a whole network of previously invisible trails. Here was one used by a red squirrel as it carried black walnuts off to who knows where. Here was the path of a mouse or vole, always passing next to or under downed logs. The damp evidence of a freshwater seep where snow melted on contact. I half expected to see preordained pathways for each snowflake as they fell.

Flowers, too, provide a sort of trail for those that know where to look. It's obvious to us why insects will choose to be attracted to certain flowers – they're just such pretty colors, or they produce such intoxicating smells (or, simply smells, as is the case with the *Rafflesia*, an Indonesian plant sometimes known as "Corpse Plant" for the rotten flesh smell that it produces.) But when viewed under ultraviolet light, a wavelength visible to many insects, flowers reveal flashing neon sign level enticements to pollinators. "Free drinks inside!"

I remember being in awe as a child when I first realized that I could conceivably get to anywhere in the country by simply following the correct series of paths. My front door was connected to every front door in America by pavement, cinders, packed dirt, or asphalt. And anywhere you couldn't drive, you could walk. If you couldn't walk, you could swim. Nature has dissected the landscape with so many pathways, and we have added so many more, often paving over those that nature had first laid down. If there's a place you want to be, whether it's a mountain meadow in Wyoming, a beach in Bali, or a dive bar downtown, there's a trail that leads there.

# Pressing Matters

The opening weekend of archery season found me sitting in a blind with two of my kids, full of coffee, high hopes and great expectations. A child's ability to sit in the manner required for an archery hunt has an inversely proportionate relationship with the amount of time they are required to do so. This poses a conundrum for a hunting mentor and father. On the one hand, there are lessons about patience and perseverance, the character building that comes from learning how to embrace suffering, not to mention the possibility of meat on the table. On the other hand, they were young kids and I wanted them to enjoy this. They would have the rest of their lives to suffer. We packed up and headed back to the house. It was 7:30 AM.

What do you do when faced with a warm afternoon and hours to kill before the evening hunt? You trick your kids into helping you out with a "fun new activity." The fall of 2018 saw a bumper crop of apples.

You'd think the etymology of bumper crop would have something to do with a truck so laden with harvest that the bumpers dragged on the ground, or that you couldn't walk through an orchard without bumping into a few apples. I like those two, but the real story is that the word bumper was used in the sixteen hundreds to refer to a large wine glass. Bumper then simply came to mean a large amount of anything. Now you know. Anyways, in what has become a pattern of me spending way too much time and energy for something that I'm really not that interested in to begin with, I decided that the time was ripe to make some apple cider. How hard could it be?

The first step, locating the cider press. My father had spoken of an old crusher and press combination that they used to use as kids that was likely stored in a barn near my grandmother's house, maybe a fifteen-minute drive away. The old man's memory was accurate, and there in a corner of an old outbuilding, under three inches of dust and cobwebs, stood the press. A monstrously heavy contraption of metal the density of dark matter mounted atop of a base constructed of timbers that must have come from the great redwood forests. Despite the weight and sturdiness of the individual components, the whole thing looked as though it might crumble like a Nature Valley granola bar if you blinked too forcefully. There was a chain that looked like it came off the USS Constitution wound tightly around everything, struggling to maintain the fight against gravity and entropy. There was also a very yellow but very non-movable VW Beetle blocking the way.

Over the course of the next couple hours we shifted, jacked up, pushed, pulled, cursed, and otherwise cajoled the press out from behind fifty years of the kinds of things that accumulate in an old barn. Getting the press into the bed of the truck in one piece took similar effort. As did unloading it without the whole thing disassembling itself in a moment of furious, spontaneous disintegration. No matter, we were in business.

Step two, collecting some apples. A good cider, I'm told, is made from a blend of different apple varieties. I couldn't tell you what kind of apples we had on the property – there were some red ones and some green ones and some that were full of holes and bite marks, so we figured it best to get some of each. Collecting the apples didn't take long – pull the tractor up to a tree, raise the bucket, shake the tree a bunch, repeat. In less than an hour we had probably twenty-five gallons worth of apples, supplemented by some leaves, twigs, and bugs of various description.

The crusher half of the cider press had a metal hopper that you'd load the apples into, with a large toothed gear that would smash the apples and drop the pieces into a wooden basket below. The wheel to turn the gear had no handle, so a pair of vice-grips was clamped to it in order to give some leverage. Turn the wheel too fast and the apples would ride across the tops of the gear teeth without getting crushed, too slow and you wouldn't be able to generate the necessary momentum to keep the thing spinning and you'd end up with an apple traffic jam. With careful calibration, apples, leaves, stems, bugs, and anything else that got too close were crushed up and dropped into the burlap-sack-lined basket.

To extract the juice, a hydraulic jack was placed on top of a board on the basket and jacked up by hand against the underside of the crusher, squeezing the crushed apples until the juice ran down a sluice board to be collected in whatever containers we had on hand. That first taste of cider, gathered in cupped hands as it ran off the sluice board, still warm from the sun, was incredible. I have this thing, and I know I'm not the only one, that everything tastes better when you cook or consume it outside, and that when it's something that you've grown or harvested yourself it only makes it that much better. Potatoes from the grocery store are okay, ones from the farmer's market are better. Potatoes you dig yourself rank higher, and the only way to top that is to dig ones that you've planted yourself. By that measure, this was the best apple cider I'd ever encountered. I suppose it was technically still apple juice at this point, since it doesn't become cider until some level of fermentation had occurred, but whatever. It was good.

Straight from the source sampling didn't last long, because within minutes there was a swarm of yellowjackets hovering around the press, alighting on the sodden burlap liner in the basket, and drowning in the outflow. Each pot and panful that was collected had to be filtered of sodden insect bodies before being dumped into empty gallon jugs, growlers, and two-liter bottles. The end result was about seven gallons of fresh pressed, soon-to-be cider.

After allowing the containers to sit for a few days, we had a product that could truly be called cider. I figured at this point pasteurizing would be a good idea. This stops the action of the naturally occurring yeast and bacteria, preventing further fermentation and killing off the bacteria, some of which could potentially be harmful. Now *not* pasteurizing means that in the right conditions, you could produce hard cider, something I'm keen to try eventually, but for now we were keeping things under-21. The cider was heated in a large stock pot until it hit 160° and then cooled, jarred, and frozen.

The final result was . . . okay. It kind of had a fresh cut grass taste to it, less like the sweet product straight off the press. I don't know if the pasteurization process caused some kind of change to the sugars, or if maybe some "bad" apples got into the mix and were only now making their presence known, but there was a little bit of a letdown, especially since the initial taste test produced such great results. Apple cider is funny, it's one of those things that, were we to buy a couple gallon jugs at the store, the first half gallon would be gone before the groceries were put away, and the rest of it by the next day. Cravings satisfied, that second jug might sit for several weeks before someone finally says "Oh yeah, cider!" The homemade version worked in a similar fashion. My wife wasn't overly excited about the flavor to begin with, and the kids lost interest rather quickly. I now found myself staring at the six remaining gallons of cider jarred up in my freezer. I put much of it to use as a source of moisture when smoking ribs and pork shoulders, but there's still a couple gallons to deal with. I think maybe next year we switch to making moonshine.

# Intermission II

Now please don't you think me officious,
but jerky just tastes so delicious.
It's salty and tough,
and I can't get enough.
Those who don't like it make me suspicious.

# Cranial Capacity

My daughter's current obsession is dead things. Actually, at this very moment it's baby snakes, but for the last couple years it's been dead things, bones specifically, skulls more specificallier. I think most kids probably go through a similar phase at some point. First it's construction equipment, then dinosaurs, then maybe space or pirates or Legos. There are just certain things that are inherently cool and have an almost universal appeal. And animal bones certainly rank in the top ten. I'm completely behind her on this one, because it's a phase I never grew out of.

The first thing students encounter upon entering my high school classroom is a display cabinet just to the left of the entrance that's stuffed to the gills with all manner of dead things. There are bones, animal skins, pinned insects, ticks the size of your thumb preserved in jars, a bag of human teeth (I honestly don't know where that came from), feathers, a turkey foot that they like to use as a backscratcher, empty egg shells, and the crown jewel, an alligator skull given to me by a parent whose kids had outgrown their own paleontological phases.

I'm not a very organized individual, and that is reflected in the display case in my classroom. There is no order nor system to anything. Once, on a visit to the Smithsonian National Museum of Natural History, I ran into a similar scenario when I got lost looking for a restroom. Up to this point, I had been impressed by the displays, even if I found them too curated for my tastes. I ended up in a long hallway lined with wooden cases – not display cases, as everything was closed up in drawers, but what I took to be storage drawers. I thought maybe I was in a restricted area or something because of the dim light and lack of people. And so of course I opened the drawers to have a look. Each case had maybe a dozen drawers four feet long, stacked atop each other, and each drawer was filled with dead birds. There didn't seem to be any order to their arrangement. Some had tags fixed to their legs with short lengths of wire, others went unidentified. But they were all the same type of bird, or at least very closely related species. I picked one up. It was surprisingly light and incredibly soft. The colors were vivid, though I have no reference for what they looked like upon death. I can't remember what kind of birds they were, only that I was unfamiliar with them. I probably read the scientific name from one of the tags but no longer remember what the species was. Drawer after drawer, case after case, it was fascinating. The lack of formal organization made it so that I did not feel terribly bad about "handling the merchandise", though I made sure to only pick up the one and to put it back exactly as it was. Had they been more formally displayed I would not have been able to be surprised by their lack of heft. I think that explains the parental vigilance required when taking children to a place like this – there's a natural inclination to get your hands dirty. How can you know an object without touching it?

My very first year of teaching found me living in Baltimore and teaching just outside the city. I was fortunate at the time to be given my own room – oftentimes first year teachers (and beyond) are what's known as "floating" teachers, moving their supplies with them on a cart to whatever room is unoccupied during a given period. Though I had my own space, it was a small room with no display areas or counter space. This could make it difficult when it came time for labs requiring lots of materials. One such lab was on comparative anatomy. I had by this point collected several skulls from deer, raccoons, opossums, cats, and groundhogs. My uncle donated a heron skull, and I had a few other odds and ends that gave me just enough material to perform a functional lab on animal morphology. After class, a student approached me and asked if I was interested in a complete deer skeleton. Even with nowhere to keep it, I assured him that yes, if it was a clean skeleton we could definitely use it, maybe even make a class project of wiring it together.

The following Monday, before the initial bell, he and another student came up to my room toting two large black garbage bags that I supposed contained the skeleton. By the time they reached the doorway I was sure of it, as the smell of rotting deer carcass filled the small space.

"Hey, Mr. Eastman! Here you go!"

Oh, shit.

"Uh, I tell you what guys, how about we take those and put them outside, they still seem a little . . . ripe? Let's go to the parking lot and we can put them in the back of my truck."

I had to get this rotting corpse out of here before I got fired or caused a school wide shutdown for health reasons. Apparently, they thought "clean skeleton" meant "no intestines." Once outside, I peeked in one of the bags and then spent the rest of the day wondering what I was going to do with two garbage bags full of bone and hair. I'm pretty sure there was still a good amount of meat left on there too. My apartment at the time had a dumpster that was somewhat hidden from the buildings, so I figured it was the perfect place to get rid of everything. I was so anxious to be rid of the problem that I was pulled over on the way home for speeding on I-695, the Baltimore Beltway. Shit shit shit shit shit.

I sat there, forehead on steering wheel, waiting out the interminable minutes for the officer to approach. I could smell it there in the truck bed with my window down, there was no way this wasn't going to be a thing. This was like Telltale Heart level intensity. In the twenty years since that happened, I've lost the memory of exactly what went down. I do recall a hurried explanation, some degree of understanding and maybe pity, a warning (no ticket!) and a vow to never take a student at their word ever again for any reason, the lying bastards. That night after dark I dumped the two bags in my apartment complex's dumpster and washed my hands of the whole thing. And then I washed them a few more times.

So it was with complete and total understanding, and even a little enthusiasm, that I listened to my daughter explain how she wanted to start collecting skulls, and aren't they just so cool, and did I know of anywhere that we could find some. So here's where I messed up. I told her "Well, I bet if we walk through the woods we might be able to find one." Yeah, of course we would, because it just so happened that I knew where there was a woodchuck skull, and maybe we'd just "happen" upon it and she could have that little thrill of discovery for herself.

I struggle, because I think kids should experience disappointment early. Think of it as preparation for a world where disappointment is the default situation. Being able to bounce back and maintain positivity when things don't work out is a crucial skill. At the same time, as someone who kind of likes my kids and can't stand to see them suffer, I have the urge to eliminate all their frustrations and solve all their problems. So, the next time she asked to go looking for animal bones, I figured it would be a good time for her to learn that you don't always find what you're looking for.

"Can we go? Can we go? IWANNAFINDSOMESKELETONS!"

"Okay, but listen honey, it's not like they're just laying around everywhere. I think maybe we were lucky the last ti . . ."

"Hey Dad, LOOK!"

Son of a bitch. There it was, a raccoon skull and part of a spine laying just off the edge of the trail. Next came the skull of a fisher, a squirrel, a bobcat, a bunch of lower leg bones from a deer that had gone unrecovered by someone the previous year. My uncle learned of her interest and gifted her two black bear skulls and a bobcat hide. The desk in her room is now overrun. There's no more space for her microscope, her hermit crab tank, or her homework.

Someday I imagine the pile of bones will be relegated to the garage, or maybe they'll find their way into my classroom collection. She might grow out of her dead animal phase and move on to something else. She might take an interest in clothes, or horses, or sports. I'm prepared for that to happen, even if I'm reluctant to admit that it's a possibility. I might lose my paleontology buddy, but hopefully only for a time. So, for now I'm just making sure that I enjoy what we've got. Even if it's 80 degrees and the sun is beating down and I've just spent three hours cutting grass and weeding potatoes and all I want to do is sit on the porch swing drinking a beer . . .

"Hey Dad, can we go look for some skulls?"

"Sure thing, honey. Just let me get my boots."

# Collector's Edition

The weekend before the start of trout season marks my annual tackle box dump and reorganization. It's a working weekend, time for respooling reels, straightening and sharpening hooks, and untangling the Gordian knot of lures that have collected in that one large tackle compartment. In addition to maintenance work, it's also a time for inventory. I'll lay out all the spinners, crankbaits, and crawfish imitators, admiring the quality and craft of each. Inline spinners get organized by size and color, the same for blade baits and soft plastics. Crankbaits don't fit into such easy categories, so they're mostly laid out in order of how much I like them. They're just nice to look at. At this point lots of people will take a photo and post it to social media so others can also marvel at their collections, though looking at pictures of someone else's lures is like looking at pictures of someone else's kids – I just can't bring myself to care that much. But I sure am enamored with my own.

Many hobbies naturally lend themselves to amassing large quantities of particular items. Some, the "collecting" hobbies like stamps or coins, seem to offer little else. I suppose with coins you could at least spend them or something, but what do you do with all those stamps? With fishing, there's at least a utilitarian aspect involved. I don't "need" that exact same crankbait in red and dark green and silver just because those colors look cool, I need them so that I can be prepared for whatever water conditions I might run into, never mind that half my lures have probably never been tied on a line. I like knowing they're there if I need them. That's what makes the big box outdoor retailers so dangerous.

A small mom and pop fly shop might have a few lures on a pegboard, but nothing that's going to break the bank (I once found a Heddon Zara Spook from what must have been 1970, still in the original package, hanging on the wall in one of these shops for $2.99.) But thanks to the hoarding instinct, a visit to someplace like Bass Pro or Cabela's could easily require a second mortgage. The variety is staggering, and for each type of bait there are five or six companies that all have their own unique takes on how to best manufacture them. You stand there, indecisive, like a kid with only five bucks to spend in the candy store, experiencing buyer's remorse before you've even made a purchase. Eventually you whittle your choices down to a reasonable number, consoling yourself with the thought that you can always come back later to round out your arsenal. No matter your purchase, you get through the checkout and there it is, the dopamine hit. That happy neurotransmitter just boppin' around up in there making you feel all good inside. Look at you go, you goofy little consumer.

Fishing is perfectly situated to exploit that kind of response. It's not like you're going to collect bass boats or dually pickup trucks with which to pull them. Most of us will be lucky to get just one of either of those things. But a six, seven, eight-dollar lure? That's not unreasonable at all. It's super reasonable, so reasonable I may as well grab a few more. Man, that feels good.

As reasonable as tackle prices may be, continually adding to your collection can still get expensive. That's part of the reason I decided I was going to make my own lures. There are some really talented people out there making some incredibly detailed crankbaits, and they're often kind enough to film the process and put it out there for free so that everyday folks like me can get their hopes up only to wind up making total fools of themselves. It's kind of like watching a Bob Ross tutorial.

"Your happy trees look more like sad gargoyles."

"But he makes it look so easy!"

Some chunks of balsa wood, a few spare treble hooks, a couple of split rings and some plexiglass for a lip and I was in business. Trying to go with a natural-ish flash, I decided on aluminum foil for the sides, embossing some scales with a dull pencil. A little bit of glue, a black sharpie for contrast, and I had it, my first crankbait. It kind of looked like someone had left a package of Swedish fish in the sun and then tried to reshape it before sticking it in the fridge to cool. And then colored it with a black sharpie. A little bit of five-minute epoxy painted on the outside and it was ready for testing.

It floated, and when pulled through the water it had a kind of wounded fish, side-to-side motion to it. I was happy with it for a first attempt, though it was immediately clear that I would need to do a bit more collecting before I could make one that I would be proud of. I needed a shopping list.

Airbrush kit.

Split ring assortment and plier set.

Hooks in every imaginable size and color.

Airbrush paint and cleaner.

Slow curing epoxy.

Disposable craft brushes.

Wire for making eyelets.

Lead for proper buoyancy control.

Holographic fish eye stickers

Rotary tool bit assortment for carving blanks.

And of course, every little purchase came with its own dose of brain stimulating neurotransmitters. I'd only made one crankbait at this point and already I was hooked.

When the weather is too cold or the water too high, I'll sometimes head down to the basement and tinker with little fish-shaped blocks of wood. I've gone from total novice that makes crappy lures to a guy with lots of experience who makes crappy lures. I've given a few away; one even managed to catch a bass, though I would credit the angler and not the lure in that instance. I've tried fishing, unsuccessfully, with a few of the different baits I've made. A few more that didn't work out so well but still looked good are mounted in a display box in my sunroom. But that *first* lure I made? That one has never seen the water of a lake, pond, river, or stream. It hangs over my workstation, there in the basement. An original. A one of a kind. A collector's edition.

# Reflection

Growing up, my childhood friends and I got up to all the usual things that kids do when they have an endless summer and no supervision. Of all the stuff you could do to kill some time, there was one thing, I wouldn't call it an "activity" exactly, that seemed to be our first choice whenever possible.

"Wanna go down to the creek?"

The water exerted an irresistible, inescapable pull, but instead of the songs of sirens, we were drawn by the promise of frogs, salamanders, and crayfish. All manner of interesting things could be found by simply flipping a few rocks and waiting for the silt to settle. Occasionally you'd be able to capture a couple of large crayfish, and then, bound by ancient adolescent male codes, would be compelled to construct an arena where you'd pit them against one another in a brutal fight to the death. Usually they would just scuttle under the rocks that encircled the ring, disappearing from view. It reminds me of that Far Side cartoon where two aliens have captured a couple of astronauts and one alien says to the other, "Shake the jar and see if they'll fight!"

If there were no creepy crawlies to be found, or once we got bored watching them sit there not fighting each other, we'd usually turn to the next best thing: dam building. We'd lay out a row of large stones, working like Egyptian masons, attempting to make them fit together seamlessly. Handfuls of sand and mud were then packed against the upstream face, our thinking being that the small particles would sift into any cracks and seal them up. If you were really good, and really patient, you could sometimes back up enough water that it would spread out and flow around the edges of the dam. At this point, a large flat rock was the go-to tool for digging out a large pool above the dam, the goal being to get it deep enough that it could act as a holding pond for minnows or maybe water snakes.

The most successful dam I remember making went together much more easily and without nearly as much work. My friend's house had a long, sloping backyard that ended with a drop off into a gully maybe three feet across and about as deep. There was a stream that ran through, but the streambed was mostly sand and mud, lacking the kind of rocks and ledges that made a stream interesting. This day, though, we found a large piece of corrugated fiberglass in the woods behind the stream, maybe blown off of an adjacent construction site, that would turn an uninteresting stream into a very interesting stream very quickly. We were able to flex the fiberglass sheet so that it would fit between the banks of the gully and then sank it in the mud. We spent maybe ten minutes packing mud against the edges, impressed with the force of the little bit of water that had already begun to collect above it. A few long logs propped on the downstream side kept the whole thing upright, and, being ten, we admired our handiwork and went back up the hill to his house to eat microwaved pizza rolls and try in vain to find his father's pornography stash.

Sometime later, ten minutes, an hour - I don't know, it was a long time ago – we went back to the backyard only to find the bottom of the lawn completely underwater. The dam had been so successful that the stream had entirely filled the gully, spilling over the banks into not only his yard, but those of several soon-to-be-unhappy neighbors as well. We assumed, correctly, that simply knocking out the downstream braces would fix the whole issue, the only trouble was that the force of the water pushing against the fiberglass made moving the logs nearly impossible. After a bit of jumping and jostling, the braces began to give way. Water poured over the top of the collapsing fiberglass sheet with an intensity that neither of us had considered possible. The impounded water raced through the gully, scouring the sandy bottom and washing away sticks and rocks in a torrent the color of chocolate milk. It was impressive, and also a little scary. I don't know if any of the neighbors ever complained, but I suppose it makes sense now why his mother called me a bad influence (even if the whole thing had been his idea.)

The attraction to water is one of those universal human things. Water means life, there's no need for a complicated evolutionary explanation. Beaches, mountain streams, great waterfalls, desert oases – water attracts, captivates, and inspires us. From the hypnotic action of gently rolling ocean waves to the terrifying violence of a flash flood, there's a certain poetic parallel to mankind, a reflection of ourselves.

There are a couple of springs on the cabin property that flow in all but the driest weeks of the year. They bubble up from a hillside and meander their way down to a boggy area filled with grassy hillocks and mud holes before disappearing again underground. The area had a bulldozer taken to it in a semi-successful effort to dig out a pond. Semi-successful because there's clay, which is great at holding water, and then there's gravel, which is not. Though the pond is rarely completely dry, it's far too variable in its water level to make it a suitable habitat for fish or waterfowl. Arrive after a week of wet weather and it might reach ten feet deep at the center and cover twenty-thousand square feet. After a dry week, you'd be lucky to get your ankles wet. Hopefully one day we'll sort out the supply and drainage problems and have a proper pond, one where the kids can catch bluegill or dive off a floating platform.

Even so, the pond, such as it is, still provides endless entertainment for my kids when we visit. It's one of the first stops when going for a walk, "just to check it out." There was a wood duck with a string of ducklings hanging around this spring. I've also been seeing a mallard circling the area pretty regularly. Last week my daughter made an afternoon project of transferring tadpoles from one of the evaporating puddles to a deeper section of the pond using a mason jar. I was on the front porch, doing not much of anything, when I heard her yell.

"Hey Dad! Come here, I found something!"

"What did you find?"

"It's like some little lobsters or something!"

While we didn't end up making them fight (maybe it's a guy thing?) we did watch them intently in the hopes that they'd catch an insect or maybe one of the tadpoles. The peepers began gearing up for their evening chorus. A small stream of water bubbled and whispered, doing its best to keep the pond full.

# Rural Outfitters

Y ou can go online and buy cabin themed drink coasters made from crosscut tree branches. They're three and a half inches in diameter and you can pick up a set of six for $27.99. There's upcycled pallet slats artisanally hand painted with various animal tracks, poster prints outlining a list of cabin rules like "No alarm clocks allowed" and "Nap Often", personalized "Welcome to _____'s Cabin" wall hangings. Sixteen dollars will get you a set of four tree branches that have been specially cut and drilled to serve as wall hooks. Everything strives to hit just the right notes of comfort and relaxation while trying to maintain some of that sweet, sweet mountain-man cachet.

I suppose cabin furnishings are no different than those of any other dwelling. As in, commercial America has no reason not to cash in on this little corner of the home décor market. There's certainly a particular aesthetic, one heavy with flannel, natural woods, and antler-based hardware. It just all feels so . . . forced? Farced? I suppose there's nothing wrong with wanting to make your space cozy and comfortable. To each their own, live and let live, etc., but it feels like furnishing a cabin in such a fashion is more appropriate for a Pottery Barn or Pier 1 catalog shoot than a retreat to the woods. Yeah, I guess I'm gatekeeping cabin décor.

A proper cabin has to have a fireplace. That's not up for debate. In my view, a good fireplace has a large chimney wall faced with stone, preferably sourced from the surrounding land. Maybe a mantlepiece from an equally local source, be it a large timber salvaged from a burned-out barn or a rough shaped chunk of granite. The mantlepiece might hold a few assorted knickknacks, an antler shed found on the property, perhaps a stuffed pheasant that was shot by someone's grandfather, an arrow point turned up during plowing. Things reflective of the local environment. If it was mass produced in a factory, can it really have any meaning or value?

I've been in a number of cabins that have framed art hanging on the walls. Some had colorful vistas or vibrant sunset photos, some frames held prints of majestic wildlife. They felt an awful lot like things you might find in a hotel room. The ones that caught my eye, though, were the frames containing maps. Artwork that anchored the viewer in relation to their surroundings. I was able to go online and order a print of the official United States Geological Survey topographical map for the quadrant where my cabin is located. The dirt road is identified by dotted lines, showing both the current entrance to the property as well as one that hasn't been in service for over thirty years. Black squares mark the location of buildings that no longer exist, and even the gravel pit is marked with a pair of crossed shovels as though it contained buried treasure. The highest point on the property appears to be at 1730 feet above sea level according to the contour lines. It increases to a maximum height of 1772 feet on the neighboring property. It's a cool map, one that I intend to frame and display at some point, but something about the glossy new feel doesn't hit quite the right note. I think I want the map for the area that was hand drawn a hundred years ago and sat in a local library's damp basement archives for a while, darkened crease lines, worn edges, faded ink and all. Maybe I'm too picky.

No cabin is complete without some display of hunting prowess commanding center stage. We have the perfect location in ours for a shoulder mount of a majestic bull elk. The only problem, there are no elk here. I suppose I could pay for a guided elk hunt in a western state and bring my trophy back and display it proudly, which I would probably do, but this is not elk country, and therefore this is not an elk cabin. No, pride of place belongs to the whitetail that I'm going to get. The whitetail that is born here, that feeds itself from the beans that I plant here. Someday. Cabins in the northeast might reserve that place for old lobster traps and rigging lines. If you're in Alaska, maybe a grizzly mount. But it should definitely be locality based.

A magazine cabin always has a professional style kitchen, ten-burner gas range, stainless steel wine refrigerator, indoor brick oven. A lived-in cabin has a bunch of mismatched dishes from a thrift store and five hundred coffee mugs. I suppose if your cabin comes with a professional chef, then a professional kitchen is a no brainer. If, however, you're not vacationing at a celebrity ski lodge, then you might make do with bacon and eggs fried in an old cast iron skillet. The most available cast iron, at least in my area, is from the Lodge Cast Iron Company. There's a reason it's called that. In addition to mismatched cookware, flatware, and drinkware, we've also got mismatched Tupperware. That's because whenever something at home gets upgraded, the old stuff is brought up to the cabin to begin its second life.

Bedrooms in cabin magazines are like something out of Swiss Family Robinson. Soft yellow string lights hang along bunkbeds constructed from peeled logs. Mortise and tenon joinery abounds. There's maybe even an antique draw knife and hatchet hung on the walls to complete the look. The beds in our cabin are whatever we could get our hands on. After all, if I'm in bed I'm sleeping, and I don't much care how the frame looks. My chief concern is that there's enough space for me to move over when my dogs inevitably decide that they've had enough of the floor and jump up to join me. I may discourage it, but I really do kind of like that part.

Look up "cabin porch" and you'll undoubtedly see picture after picture of wooden rocking chairs, hurricane lanterns, and artfully placed fleece throw blankets. We've got a rocking chair. It says "Craft Shop" across the top in routed letters. It does not match the porch swing, which is green, rickety, and uncomfortable. There's a decrepit Weber grill that gets brought out from time to time, and one of those green reflective metal signs that denotes a hiking trail that I "rescued" one day many years ago. But the porch is out of the sun during the warmest parts of the day, and it provides a comfortable place to lie down as evening comes on. It also provides the perfect vantage point to shoot at groundhogs, if you're into that sort of thing.

So if you are fortunate enough to have a cabin, or have a place to put a cabin, or are in a position to think about purchasing land on which to put a cabin, and you're looking for advice on the best ways to outfit your living space, here you go. Do what you want. Don't let a magazine, website, or catalog tell you what looks good. And don't let some cranky guy that wrote an essay about it tell you either. Maybe your cabin is deep in the pine forests of Maine. Perhaps it's a detached shed in a Wisconsin suburb. Maybe your cabin getaway is a rooftop garden above a high-rise apartment building in New Jersey, or even a comfortable corner of your living room in a Nebraska farmhouse. You like the look of a Pottery Barn cabin with faux antique travel suitcases stacked in the corner? Go for it. You want to cut a canoe in half and use it as a bookshelf? Do it. You're the one who's going to be staying there, why not enjoy it?

# Placing Blame

There are certain specific days in a person's time on Earth that have a lasting impact on the rest of their life's trajectory. Many of these days are nearly universal in their occurrence. Excluding being born, seeing as how that seems to be a bit of a prerequisite, other days that come to mind include getting married, accepting a job, and having children. These all lead to a cascading series of life-altering and life-defining events. But I'm willing to bet that beyond those universal experiences, everyone has a day that, though perhaps insignificant at the time, ended up having a more lasting impact than could have possibly been imagined. For me, that day was Friday, December 18th, 2015. Secret Santa Day.

Every year the members of my department have a potluck lunch and Secret Santa gift exchange. It's annoying and stressful and fraught with potential social pitfalls. Did I get a recovering alcoholic a set of shot glasses? Is "adopt-a-goat" an acceptable charity? I don't know anything about coworker "A", will they be offended if I get them a coffee mug? One year a guy gave me a portable air compressor that plugs into your car's cigarette lighter, clearly a regifted afterthought (though it's actually been kind of useful.) This particular year, my Secret Santa got me a three pack of NAP Archery three blade mechanical broadheads.

I know, that sounds awesome, right? Only, what the hell did I know about mechanical broadheads? I'd never archery hunted in my life. I owned no archery equipment, had no archery experience, and I knew nothing about hunting deer outside of the first Monday after Thanksgiving.

"I guess you'll have to take up archery now, huh?"

I could have tucked the broadheads away somewhere and forgotten about them. I could have continued on being a one day a year hunter, heading out in the freezing weather on a Monday morning in late November to have ten or twelve hours for a single shot at a deer. But there was something intriguing about the weight of each broadhead. Something about the way the blades went from aerodynamic to potentially traumatic with just the slightest pressure. The problem here, of course, was that you can't do anything with just a broadhead. The next few months found me compulsively researching compound bows, crossbows, arrow lengths, feet per second, fixed blade vs. mechanical, I became obsessed.

I ended up going with a crossbow, as that seemed the fastest way to transition into archery from rifle. By June of that year I had purchased a crossbow, case, bolts, string wax, and rail oil. Archery season, opening much earlier in the fall, would also mean a new wardrobe. Late November at the cabin usually means temperatures topping out around 30 degrees. Early October, on the other hand, might see daytime highs in the sixties or even seventies. I'd need everything from insulating base layers to waterproof outerwear. Fluorescent orange needed to be replaced with camouflage, long underwear with moisture wicking fabrics, wool socks and 1000-gram boots with lightweight trail shoes.

Hunting during the archery season is completely different from what I was accustomed to. During the first day of rifle, especially in places like northwest Pennsylvania, deer are simply careening through the woods trying to avoid people. There's very little natural movement and every deer is on high alert. Far fewer people out and about during archery season meant that deer movements were more natural, and I'm far more interested in what deer do when they're not running for their lives. Archery also allowed for a much longer season, which had the dual effect of taking some of the pressure off (if I don't see one today there's always next week) while encouraging a deeper study of deer movement. Knowing where they were bedding, when they moved, what trails they followed, all these things became much more important during the extended archery season. I went from hoping for a chance deer encounter to studying deer behavior out of necessity. I was forced to learn more, and as a result became more intrigued by, enamored with, and connected to this animal. What was once just another animal wandering the woods became a rather important part of my weekend plans, as well as rather important part of my dinner plans.

Prior to getting into archery, I had never put in for a doe tag. What was the point? We didn't eat much venison – check that, we didn't eat any venison – and hunting to that point was more of an exercise in enduring the cold than in food procurement. I hadn't brought my children hunting, simply because they barely outweighed the .243 they'd be using if I'd brought them along. All that changed with archery. My children, 11, 8, and 5 at the time, were all comfortable firing a crossbow.

There was no scary kickback, no terrifying noise, and shots would be close enough that confidence was not an issue. Since that first year, my kids have taken four deer using those broadheads and that first crossbow. Archery allowed me to introduce my kids to a hunting lifestyle much earlier than would have otherwise been possible. They have yet to join me during rifle season, but that day is now just around the corner.

The coworker that gifted me those broadheads is someone I think of as a dear friend and an important hunting partner, despite the fact that we've never actually gone hunting together. Each morning at work we spend some time discussing the latest happenings in our hunting and fishing lives. I have no doubt she knew exactly what would happen once I opened that package, and the thousands of dollars and hundreds of hours I've since invested are a direct result of her gift of those three mechanical broadheads. I hope next year I receive some hand-tied flies – I've never been fly fishing.

# Son Number One

You ~~probably~~ definitely won't remember it, but it's a camping trip I am not likely to forget. If I was really put to it I'd guess that you were around four or five months old, but I'm notoriously bad at remembering dates. I picked four or five months because the weather was good enough that it couldn't have been winter, but not so good that the campground and state park were crowded. In fact, I don't remember seeing anyone else while we were there. Based on that, I'm going to guess late May 2005.

I packed a tent and some blankets, food, formula, and anything else that would fit in the back of the truck that might have been even a little bit useful. I remember, as fatherhood loomed ever closer, being warned about things like irregular sleep schedules and projectile vomiting, and that was just me. I couldn't imagine what would happen once you were actually born. What I don't remember being prepared for was the sheer amount of stuff that's apparently required to keep a baby alive and happy. So we left, stuffed to the rafters with any and all baby related items I could scrounge up. I was nervous, as this would be the first time we really spent "away" from home. There would be no "just handing you off for a minute so I can go to the bathroom." Your mother was nervous too, about a) being away from you for a weekend, and b) sending you off with me to hang out by roaring waterfalls and slippery cliff edges.

It was about a three-and-a-half-hour drive from Baltimore to Ohiopyle. I'm guessing you slept most of the way. We went to our usual campground and set up the tent, having our choice of the field since it was completely empty. The first day was spent playing in the sand on the beach by the river and watching the water roll by. You learned that throwing things in the water is fun, I learned that sand and diapers are natural enemies. There were frequent nap breaks, clothing changes, and dinner was formula warmed over a Coleman stove, and I think I smashed up some hotdogs for you as well. The thing I'll never forget about that first day, though, was that first night.

If ever there was a test of fatherhood, this was it. As evening came on, you began to get fussier and fussier. Your eyes got glassy and you developed a fever. Without a thermometer I had to gauge the seriousness of it using just my hand. It didn't seem that bad. Or did it? Do I pack up everything in the dark, or wait it out until morning? I don't know that I've ever missed your mother more than I did in that moment. Then the rain started. It wasn't long before the thunderclaps were drowning out the trains that passed by with regularity not two hundred yards from where we were camped. The tent began to flood. Your mother and I, being a young couple with their first child, were not yet of the means to purchase the best, or even middle of the road, in terms of quality, hence the leaks. I piled all the blankets up in the middle of the tent floor and sat atop them, rocking you back and forth while you alternated between terrifying me by crying and then terrifying me by being silent. The trains screamed and you screamed and the thunder crackled. Then, as if to test what kind of dad I might be, you developed a most aromatic case of post-digestive leakage. That remains, to this day, the longest night of my life.

Morning came, as it always does, though this one carried a little more weight to it. I had not slept more than a few minutes here and there, instead spending the whole night keeping you wrapped up and out of the water. I remember opening my eyes to the first hints of sunlight, back aching from poor posture, pants damp from the water that had seeped up through the blankets, you still swaddled in a bundle in my arms. You were finally sleeping, and you no longer felt quite so feverish. You made do with cold formula that morning, and I think I choked down a granola bar or two. I wanted nothing more than to be back home.

By the time everything was packed up, though, the sun had warmed things considerably and you were back to being a curious, babbling little human. Our route home passed by Ohiopyle Falls, and we took some time to walk down and marvel at the power of the water. Since we were already there, why not take a short hike along the loop trail? After all, how many other opportunities would we have (especially after this experience?) This was before I had a cell phone or a camera, so I don't have any pictures to commemorate the experience, but I remember very clearly you pointing at the water and rocks and clapping your hands while making happy giggling baby noises; the best kind. I counted the trip a success, and we prepared to make the long drive back home. I imagine that upon pulling up in front of the house, I handed you off to your mother and then crawled into bed and slept for three days.

We'd continue to go back to that campsite as a family for several more years, bringing along first your brother, then also your sister. It's now been a few years since we've camped in that field and stood by the river, watching the rapids roll back and collapse onto themselves. You've grown up a bit, and we don't get to spend as much time together outdoors anymore. Your work schedule (how do you have a job already?!) often means you can't come along on weekend trips to the cabin. You never really took too much interest in hunting, and Friday night halftime performances throughout the fall made it difficult to get away.

Once in a while, though, things line up perfectly, and the whole family finds the time to "unplug" together. I watch you and your brother and sister head off into the woods to embark on whatever adventure you can find, building a tire swing or testing your aim against makeshift boats in the pond.

A couple months ago you said "You know, I think I might want to try hunting this year." My initial questions was "Why?", though I didn't want to ask it for fear of making you think I was discouraging you. I instead said something like "Oh yeah? Cool." In truth, I was more excited than I had been in a long time. I'm already looking forward to our first deer hunt together, even if it means leaving at 11:30 on a Friday night after marching band, driving through the night and not getting a wink of sleep. I've had the practice, I'm ready for it.

# Getting Dirty

**E**verybody should have a garden. Whether it's a potted tomato plant growing on the back patio, a windowsill herb garden, or five acres planted with fifty different kinds of vegetables, you should take the time, if only once, to put a seed in the ground and watch it grow. Fair warning up front- it's not going to save you any time or money, in case that was important. In fact, it's going to end up costing you, but the results are more than worth it. Unless you're like me, and then the results are lots of weeds that are only good for adding volume to the compost pile. A compost pile that was supposed to make growing your own vegetables easier.

The first thing I ever grew was grass. It was at a summer camp of some sort. We were given a Styrofoam cup, some dirt, a handful of grass seeds and a black marker. The idea was to draw a face on the cup and then the growing grass would act like hair. I think the inventor of the Chia Pet went to the same summer camp.

Grass is stupid. It requires constant maintenance, doesn't produce pretty flowers, and you can't even eat it. But watching my little Styrofoam cup guy's hair grow like that was somehow the coolest thing I'd ever seen. Admittedly, I was like five and hadn't been around long enough to see too many things, let alone many cool things.

My parents had a pretty sizeable vegetable garden at the very back of their yard for as long as I remember living in that house. Each year my father would drag an antique Craftsman rototiller out from the garage and teach me swear words as he tried to get it to start. The thing looked like a horror movie torture device when it was running. I always imagined getting my foot caught in the spinning tines and then having to watch as the machine dragged me in, chopping me into vegetable fertilizer. My father would walk back and forth across the garden behind the tiller, rocking it from side to side as he went, turning over the lighter colored dry topsoil to unearth the darker layers beneath. My sisters and I followed along, picking out any large rocks, feeling the cool damp soil squish between our toes.

I always imagined that when I bought my first house I would add a garden like that. It turns out that when you only have an eighth of an acre and seven oak trees all fifty feet tall, putting in a garden is more like lumberjacking than digging. Our backyard wasn't a yard so much as it was one giant root system covered by a thin layer of poison ivy and disappointment. Acorns littered the ground simply because the squirrels couldn't dig far enough down to bury them. I settled for trying to grow lettuce in a container on the deck. Somehow the squirrels managed to make that disappear without any trouble.

Our second house had a yard more conducive to growing vegetables, but it also had rabbits. I constructed a fence. They dug under it. I buried the fence below the soil, they went up the patio stairs and jumped down from above. I eventually was able to keep them out and make a proper attempt at gardening. Inspired by pictures of lush gardens with decorative trellises and arbors, I decided on raised beds. One for peppers, one for peas, a bed for carrots, and another for lettuce and spinach. I built towers and laced string between them to give my peas somewhere to climb. I buried soaker hoses below the soil and paid actual money for actual bags of animal poop just so I could give my plants their best start. I was excited to see those first tiny sprouts emerge from the soil. I'd check their progress each day, wondering when the appropriate time was to start weeding and pruning. It turns out the appropriate time to start weeding is when you start seeing weeds grow. The tiny sprouts I had been so diligently nursing along? Weeds. So where the hell were my plants? If I squinted just right I could make out a wavy line of seedlings that were a slightly lighter color than surrounding carpet of weeds, a carpet that was looking more and more like a shag rug every day.

I bet that first carrot we dug up would have been delicious. There's no way of knowing, because it was more like a fine strand of hair than a root vegetable. But it was a start, all we needed now was patience. Patience, and many many years later, and we've gotten to a point where it makes sense to grow some things at home and other things at the cabin property. Home gardens are for herbs and lettuce, things that you want fresh but that don't keep long in a refrigerator. Camp gardens are reserved for the more low maintenance items, potatoes, carrots, onions. Last year's potato dig saw us through from October to March, stored away happily in our root cellar. The few remaining spuds that were no longer fit to consume were put into the ground two weeks ago to begin next year's crop.

Our latest planting went more smoothly than it ever has. Two hundred peppers of three varieties, several hundred potatoes and onions, pumpkins, sunflowers, bush beans, carrots, tomatoes, and corn, all done with help (voluntary!) from two of my kids. Me hoeing, one child planting, and one covering. We were done in record time. Maybe the seeds aren't spread out at exactly the proper interval, maybe the depth is a little off. There might be some beans in the corn rows, some corn mixed in with the carrots. It doesn't matter. Something will grow, and we'll all be there to harvest it, and each dinner made with it will carry the memories of hard work and sweat that went in to making it possible. Vegetables always taste better when you've got a little bit of dirt under your nails anyways.

# Oh. Canada.

When I don't get enough to eat I get cranky. When I don't get enough sleep, I get surly. And when I don't have regular intervals of extended time outdoors, I get this weird combination of depressed, angry, anxious, and distracted. Time outdoors, of course, means more than simply existing in an unbounded space. I'm talking about getting out, away from people. My daily dog walks don't quite cut it – sure, I get to walk along the river, and there's even a couple hundred yards of trail that pass beneath a railroad bridge where there's some closed canopy and an almost wild feel, but there's always the inescapable background noise of life there as well. Train whistles, traffic, the dredge boat in the middle of the river dropping its huge iron claw at regular intervals. People and their barking dogs, my dogs barking at their dogs, them grumbling about my dogs barking at their dogs. It's like using school glue to close a wound: It might work, but it's not a long-term solution.

A state park will do in a pinch, bonus points if it's big enough and remote enough that I don't have to see any other cars in the parking lot. The experience is dampened slightly by the necessary highway drive to get there, but it is possible to lose yourself for a few hours. But I imagine that to someone starved for wilderness, a few hours in a state park is like a single shot of whiskey to a recovering alcoholic – it's everything you ever wanted, but it's also worse than nothing at all. Every few years finds me getting antsy for an extended wilderness trip, one where you can really forget about everything and immerse yourself in the outdoors. The kind of trip I'm talking about has the same effect on the spirit as power washing has on years of built up grime on a concrete sidewalk. After moving back to Pennsylvania, I had been too busy and had gone too long without such a trip. And so, on October 13th, 2016, I posted the following message on Facebook to a close group of friends.

> *I've been reading a lot lately. Muir, Leopold, Abbey, Thoreau, etc. I'm struck by the evocative descriptions of pristine wilderness and untouched places. Cracked and broken desert canyons, frigid Alaskan rivers, untainted New England forests. I'm sad that I can't experience those places as they were a hundred or more years ago. I'm sadder still that my kids have even less of a chance to see places unshaped by human activity. Short of a very expensive trip to the interior of Russia or China, or perhaps the Australian outback, I think the dream of witnessing the world "before man" is one that will remain entirely between my ears. I have, however, been lucky enough to catch a brief glimpse in places like the wilderness areas of Wyoming, the*

*Moose River in Maine, and a couple places in Canada that have a strange sort of claim on whatever part of my heart or soul or whatever that finds me returning there in my mind more and more frequently. I'm sure you've all heard of "Shinrin-yoku", the Japanese idea of a Forest Bath, letting the natural world remove the mental pressures of whatever you would call the world we live in now. I've got to get out, and I've got to make sure my kids have the chance to get out. To see what I've seen, to experience things that most American children probably never will. I know a few young explorers who would jump at the chance to live, temporarily at least, without the electronic tether, the unnatural blue-glow aura of the screen, the hyperscheduling. Hell, who wouldn't? I think most of us, with the exception of a very lucky few, don't get nearly enough forest baths in our lifetime. We need a trip. For some this may be one of the last opportunities, and for others it may be the first installment in a lifetime of adventuring. Nature can only do so much, though. It's the setting, the backdrop, for what makes the trip truly an experience. As much as I might remember a specific portage trail, wide open sky, or that one particular log that stuck out from Turner's Falls at a funny angle, looking for all the world like it wanted to catch ahold of an aluminum Grumman and rip it end to end, it's the people that were there that I remember most. I might think "that was a nice waterfall", but I'm more likely to remember Timmy washing his jeans on a stick, or Fred sending Buckner's mess kit tumbling over the edge. Getting yelled at by Natalie for leaving the rental van a terrible mess or rigging a sail to up to two canoes in an effort to save a little strength. It's only going to happen if it's planned, and planned early. Clear some calendar space, save some sick days, buy one less café grande latte mocha sugar injection. Find out who was left off this list and invite them. We'll need people on this trip. Some capable of telling a story, some able to haul weight, others to teach first timers the art of knife sharpening, walleye gutting, backpaddling like crazy because you didn't realize you overshot your take-out and are hurtling towards, if not certain death, then at least a complete and thorough soaking. Start now. Let's plan dates, locations, crew members. My vote is Kipawa, mid to late June. Unless that's a bad time. Then July. Or maybe August. Whatever works.*

The response was immediate and unified. I guess I'm not special when it comes to feeling the tug of the outdoors. There were comments enthusiastically voicing support, questions about logistics, and an offer from my mother to buy a sandwich ring from the local grocery store so we could meet at her house to begin planning (I was really hoping to do the planning at a place that served pub fries and beer, but how do you turn down a sandwich ring from your own mother?)

After much round and round and back forth, eighteen of us committed to making a trip into Quebec to a location that several of us were familiar with. We planned canoe routes, meal preparation, camp chores, fishing licenses, and transportation. Now all we needed to do was find nine floatable canoes and a way to haul them and we'd be on our way. The trip participants included my father, my oldest sister and her two oldest boys, me and my two oldest kids, four people who were directly responsible for teaching me about whitewater boating as well as a few of their own kids, one of my closest high school friends and his son, and a father/daughter duo we picked up on the way there.

Five or six of us had done this trip before, some as many as five times (this would be my fourth.) This one, though was different. My first trip was when I was in seventh grade, which would put me right around 13 years old. I made another trip in high school at around 16, and one more in my late twenties. This trip saw me staring at forty and what's more, someone thought that since it was my idea, I was by default in charge of logistics. Allow me just a moment to explain how utterly insane that idea is. I'm great at getting stuff done. I suck at figuring out what needs to be done. This might explain why we spent a week that first Saturday afternoon trying to sort out our out-of-country fishing licenses in the cramped entryway of a Kipawa ZEC housetrailer. The memory of those three sweaty hours has been intentionally erased, but I do recall my father going behind the "official" desk to sort everything out since the very pleasant but not so very competent agent was having difficulty figuring out what it was we were after.

Permits in hand (turns out you could do it all in advance online, if only someone competent was running the show), we hit the dirt/gravel/sand road for a couple hours of leisurely travel. We had four cars in our caravan, and avoiding the dust kicked up by those in front meant we were spread out over about two miles. When official directions include phrases like "turn at the seventh logging camp" you can't exactly afford to lose sight of your lead car. The trip was an approximation of what we call a "loop-trip" – one that ends where it started. These are popular because they don't require running a shuttle, so your take-out point is the same as your put-in. I say this was an approximation because there were seven miles separating the two ends of our trip. We decided that rather than running a shuttle, since there was no good spot to leave a vehicle at the put-in, we'd drive all the cars to the takeout. I would then shuttle all the drivers back to the put-in, then drive the last vehicle back to the take-out, where I was supposed to hop on a mountain bike we had brought along and bicycle my way once more back to the put-in. I would lock the bike to a convenient tree and we'd pick it up on the way out. Sounded like a great plan. Seven miles is nothing.

The seven-mile bike ride turned into a twenty-minute delay trying to even get the chain to spin. I would normally just give up and go do something else, but that option had been removed. Once I got the bike working it was a simple matter of making my way back. Something funny about me (not really funny "ha-ha", more funny-pathetic) is that I have zero sense of direction. I'm convinced it's a genetic trait since no amount of studying or working has helped me to improve it. I didn't get lost on the bike ride back, only because there was just one turn I had to make, but it made me nervous enough that I couldn't really settle into any sort of rhythm. The other thing that made the establishment of a rhythm impossible was that I was trying to bike back over four or so inches of soft, fine sand. Biking was more work than walking, especially on the uphill sections. So I spent a good bit of time pushing this bike along a deserted logging road. I had been begging to get away from other people, hoping the whole drive up that we wouldn't see any other canoers or campers on our trip, and now all I wanted was for someone to show up and give me a lift. No one did. A win, I guess?

It made sense to ride rather than walk on the downhill sections, this should at least be a breeze. Except that backcountry Canadian logging roads are more like a maze of gulleys interspersed with pointy rocks that would make any bladesmith jealous. I'd get the front wheel stuck in a track and had no choice but to follow it wherever it led, usually into a thicket of tangled knife-like plants on the side of the road. After one particularly spectacular crash, I swear I heard the huffing of a bear from an uncomfortably close distance. I jumped on the bike and sprayed sand behind me, legs churning madly but making no progress, like something from a cartoon. Nearly two hours and several gallons of sweat later, I eventually managed to make it back to the put-in.

Where was everybody? Where were the boats? Where was the food and water? Seriously, I needed water. Sixteen of the seventeen remaining people had left, striking out towards our first portage. Left behind was Greg, mid-twenties and in great shape, who was to provide some much-needed paddle power that would rejoin us with the rest of the group. I would never in a million years have thought that a crew of sixteen people, spanning ages from 7 to 67, would be able to get such a jump on two healthy fit guys in the prime of their lives, but it was hours before we came within sight of them. We caught up to the group right around the time that things started to go really, really wrong.

Reunited, I regaled everyone with tall tales of desert excursions and bear encounters, happy to be back and eager to hear if anyone had seen anything more exciting than sand in the last few hours. We had just arrived at the first portage of the trip. I'd actually been looking forward to this, the chance to teach my boys how to strap on a pack and make your way cross country. I also felt I still had something to prove to everyone else (to myself?) in terms of toughness and work ethic. Based on the maps, there should have been a trail leading over the hill to the next lake. I recalled the portage from the last time we had done the trip, only four of us then. That had been eleven years ago. There was a faded piece of flagging tape hanging from a tree limb, it could only be the marker for the trailhead. We spent the next hour or so wandering around looking for anything that resembled a passage through the forest, but it seems that time passes quicker in the Canadian wilderness, and all traces of a trail had been obliterated. A failure of that magnitude on the first day was not a good omen.

I'm not a believer in fate or destiny, so let's call it a fortuitous setback. After being unable to locate a portage trail, we decided that backtracking was our best option. I say fortuitous because our original route may have proven far too difficult for the age and experience of a lot of the group, and we established a new route that would reduce the number of portages and give us an extra layover day – when you camp in the same location for more than one night in a row. We paddled back to our original put-in and worked backwards through a series of lakes looking for a place to camp for the night. We ended up spending that first night camped in a turnout off the side of a logging road. It wasn't ideal or picturesque, but it was dry, level ground. Surprise, surprise, logging roads, even in the middle of nowhere in Canada, are still roads. And roads carry vehicles (except when you need a ride, apparently.) Why those vehicles were driving there at ninety miles an hour at three-thirty in the morning I'll never know, but we all fortunately awoke un-run-over the following morning.

We spent a leisurely afternoon paddling across lakes and eating gorp by the gallon Ziploc bagful. Gorp, or trail mix, supposedly gets its name from the ingredients. Depending on who you talk to, it either stands for "Good Old Raisins and Peanuts", or "Granola, Oats, Raisins, and Peanuts." I guess a more accurate term for what I carried would be "CRAMP", cashews, runts, almonds, m&ms, and pineapple (dried, of course.) The weather held up and we enjoyed ourselves immensely. The big draw of this trip was always the descent of the Kipawa River, ending at a spot called "Turner's Falls", an impassable waterfall that drops maybe forty feet in two stages. It's a great place to camp since large boulders form a naturally protected kitchen area, there are plenty of level tent sites, and the constant turbulence from the waterfall keeps the mosquitoes and blackflies to a minimum.

This time, though, there would be no descent of the river. We would be approaching from the other direction since our first day change of plans. This meant paddling upstream through a couple of decent rapids, with no guarantee that when we arrived the spot wouldn't already be claimed by another group. Early in the morning, Greg and I set out again carrying only some off-brand pop tarts, a tent, and a couple large, bright yellow dry bags. We paddled hard for maybe four miles and arrived on the beach below the waterfall. There were canoes, some packed, some not, and voices from up the trail. The big question then, was, are these people just leaving, or did they beat us by mere minutes? It was a group of about a dozen girls, and it became quickly clear that they were packing up and heading down the river that we had just paddled up. We asked if they minded us stashing some gear to claim the spot. They were cool with it, so we set up a tent and hung the yellow dry bags in a conspicuous location. We then raced back downstream, running a rapid we probably shouldn't have, and pulled up on the beach at our last campsite. Everyone had already packed up in anticipation of us hitting the jackpot, and all eighteen of us were soon off again, once more back up the river. What followed was three days of lounging around, goofing off, sleeping late, and eating like kings.

One of the more bizarre rituals that has developed on these kinds of trips with these kinds of people is the "formal dinner" night. Checkered tablecloth, candles, steaks that we'd been lugging around packed in twenty or thirty pounds of dry ice for the last four or five days; we had it all. And formal also means dressing up. Some go the thrift store route, looking for the most ostentatious finds like old wedding dresses or bright purple tuxedos. I'll admit to almost buying a camel hair dinner jacket for five dollars, but the thought of packing all that weight in and back out was too burdensome. Somebody even brought along a solar oven in order to make fresh bread. The dry ice was broken up and added to containers of "bug juice" (basically Kool-Aid, the best flavor is blue, by the way), giving it a soda-like quality, and I may have also packed in a couple bottles of Southern Comfort to add to the mix.

When close to the falls, the roar of the water made conversation difficult. This forced anyone standing nearby to just stop and appreciate, and listen. If my estimate is correct, I've spent nine nights of my life falling asleep to the sound of that particular waterfall, and on all nine nights I slept like a baby dosed with horse tranquilizers. I'm not a huge fan of fish, but I'll eat it on occasion. The best fish of my life, in fact one of the best meals of my life, came from the waters below Turner's Falls. The turbulent outflow is a great spot for catching walleye, and that's just what we did. Someone would catch one, it would be knocked on the head and then tossed up onto the rocks above the falls where it was filleted, seasoned, and fried. Total time from hooked to cooked was ten minutes. Maybe it was good because it was so fresh, maybe it was good because we were starving. It didn't matter. The only meal to ever rival that was the first bacon cheeseburger on the drive back home. After a couple of days with nothing to do but whatever we wanted, it was time to hit the take-out and head for home. As though waiting out our good time, the last day was a soaking wet affair of rain and clouds. I remember that we left the bike at the put in, but we took the lock with us.

There were less than ideal moments on that trip, of course. But whenever I look back on something that I wish to remember in a positive light, those moments fade into the background. Memory is funny that way. When you've had a miserable day and finally get home, you regale your spouse or roommate or cat with an itemized list of all the mounting atrocities and injustices that explain why you're in the mood you're in. Anything positive that happened that day gets buried and forgotten. I hope that my boys retain the memories of the good times they had on that particular trip, and I need for them to remember it in a positive light. It's been a few years since I've been out, and I'm getting that itch again. But I'm also getting older. I'm going to need some canoeing partners to help shoulder the load.

# Close Calls

U ntil I began really spending time at the cabin property, I was unaware of the fact that there are trees, and then there are trash trees. As far as I can figure, a trash tree is a variety that doesn't have economic value. If there's a cherry tree growing amongst a stand of a dozen poplars, you sacrifice the poplars for the sake of the cherry. There's a market for cherry – no one wants veneer made out of poplar. It's apparently not even good as firewood, since it burns up too quickly and doesn't throw off a lot of heat. Guess which one our property has lots of.

It's not enough to be a tree of the proper pedigree, though, A tree must also be straight, mature, and free from defects. A tree of the proper age, species, and shape might be worth a thousand dollars. A valuable specimen like an oak might be worth nothing if it has a hollow spot or a curved trunk or multiple tops. It's funny, because most of my "favorite" trees on the property aren't worth the energy needed to cut them down. Their value, to me, is not measured in board feet. There's this one crazy looking maple tree at least fifteen feet around at the base. There's not much of a top to it since it's dead. All the upper limbs have long since fallen off, and there's a great hollow running all the way to the top of what's left. There's one dead branch that looks a bit like a claw reaching up, just waiting for the day that it, too, succumbs to decay and gravity. I like it for several reasons. First, it's a reminder of how big these things can get if given the time – there aren't many other trees on the property that can rival it in circumference. For as long as I've been around that tree has been dead, standing silent vigil alongside the logging road. I can't imagine what it looked like when it was in its full glory. It's also got a mysterious, spooky charm to it – fledgling vultures have been known to hang out on the one remaining branch, really rounding out that haunted house feel. It also serves as a handy landmark when trying to give directions to someone who is not yet familiar with the lay of the land.

"Go until you get to the dead maple tree and then climb the hill."

"How will I know which one is the dead maple?"

"You'll know."

Other trees I like for their shade, or for their ability to produce apples. Some are good climbing trees that give you another perspective on things when you're in the uppermost branches, swaying with each breath of wind. There is one tree that I think about more than any other, though. It's not there anymore, and I really never noticed it until the last minutes of its life.

The tree in question was a medium sized cherry tree, split at the top, branched in such a way as to make it worthless as far as lumber. It sat, along with a smattering of other spindly trunks, at the top corner of the field directly in front of the cabin, and my father had decided that it was time for it to go. We began by cutting the smaller trees from around it, opening up a space for us to work. He'd cut, I'd haul out. We make a pretty efficient team in most things, I've learned to anticipate his movements and we have kind of a seamless dance that we do when working together. The first hint that this day was different came when I was picking up one of the downed trees, a small one that was easily dragged out, and I found myself face down in the dirt. I like to think that it was because he was so used to me paying attention to what he was doing that he didn't think twice about cutting the next tree while my back was turned. It caught me square in the back of the head, dropping me to the ground. It was only a small tree, nothing serious, and I was able to gain my feet after only a brief moment of shock and some dizziness. Like I said, that should have been enough signal from the universe to say "Okay, time's up!" If we had quit then, there wouldn't be much of a story here now.

Once all the small trees had been cleared from the area and piled up, it was time to tackle the cherry. It was no different than any of the other dozens of trees we had felled. It wasn't especially big, it was not rotten inside (which can pose serious problems when cutting.) No, just a run of the mill tree.

"I'll drop it in the road and then we'll haul it over to the pile."

That should have been it, I should have said "Okay." And then we would have been done.

"Why not cut it so it falls the other direction, then it's on the pile already and we won't have to drag it anywhere. It'll be easier." I was always looking for an easier way.

I think maybe the fact that my father agreed to this should have been an indication that he had begun to value my opinion and judgement. I was no longer just expected to follow orders, I was a part of the team that had some input. That should be a great accomplishment. What I really wish is that he would have just called me an idiot and done whatever he wanted like usual. But this time, of all the times he could have listened to me, this was the time he picked.

When an NFL coach makes a gutsy call, there are two potential outcomes. He's either hailed as a genius hero on Monday morning, or he's torn apart by critics and fans as the worst coach in history. Everything is results dependent. I could have been a genius hero if I wasn't such an idiot. Despite my father's initial assessment of the situation, he began to cut the tree in such a way that it would fall onto our slash pile, just as I had suggested.

I don't have a clear memory of how it happened, but a few things remain pretty distinct. I remember him yelling "run!", and then I remember running. I recall my left elbow straightening out and then continuing on past 180° to the point that I slapped myself on the back-left shoulder in a way that even Gumby would find impossible. I don't know if I ran into something or if I got hit by the falling tree or if my radius and ulna had a temporary out of body moment, but something was now really wrong. I turned to see him pinned beneath the tree, a large branch laying across his knee – the one that had just been surgically replaced a couple months prior.

"I'm gonna need you to grab the saw and cut me out."

He said it so calmly that I freaked out a little bit more. I tried to grab the power saw only to find that my left arm was unusable. The most distinct memory of the whole ordeal for me is using my foot to hold the chainsaw trigger by pushing up with my toes and then using my right arm to pull the cord in order to get the saw started. I laid it across the log and had to thump my now useless left hand onto the saw to provide a little balance. I was about halfway through the branch when the cut caused the weight to begin shifting, and he told me to stop. At this point it didn't matter, because the chain of the saw was now solidly pinched in the kerf of the cut.

"Go get help."

I started the truck and tore down the driveway to the dirt road at speeds reserved for interstate highways, laying on the horn the whole time. My uncle has a place right nearby, so I careened up his driveway, still holding down the horn with my elbow. He was not home, but his girlfriend was. I think it was she who called 911. I laid down in the gravel driveway, the full pain finally settling in. An ambulance/pickup-truck hybrid arrived and they told me to get in the back, but I tried explaining that it was my father, on the next property over, who was the one that needed attention.

"Nah, he's fine" they told me.

Apparently the ground was still soft enough after a recent rain that his leg wasn't completely crushed. The branch also happened to have the slightest curve that meant he was only pinned, and not squashed flat like a Looney Tunes character under a steamroller. I ended up being transported to a country hospital, which is not a place you want to be. They gave me some drugs and sent me on my way, telling me not to worry. Within a day my arm was purple and yellow from wrist to shoulder. A second opinion told me I needed surgery. They cut me open, then decided that maybe I didn't need surgery after all. It was a mess.

The fallout of the whole scenario was that now whenever I use a gas-powered chainsaw, my blood pressure increases to the point where I feel like I'm going to black out. My wife also made me get a cell phone, never mind the fact that there was no reception up there to begin with. My father and uncle also had a good laugh at my expense. You'd think my opinion of my father would only have been elevated after such an ordeal - man gets crushed by tree, goes right back to work - but I can't help but question his judgement. I mean, who takes advice from an idiot like me in the first place?

# Christmas

F amily is a weird thing. You kind of assume that whatever way you grew up is similar to the way that everyone else grew up. I don't mean the specific family dynamics or the particulars of individual upbringing, more like I assumed that other families were similarly distanced. Perhaps I should explain.

My father, a native Pennsylvanian, met my mother, born in Scotland, while they were both living away from their respective home countries in Spain. An unpredictable series of events led to their eventual marriage and ultimate settling down in the Pittsburgh area. My mother's side of the family, mostly living in various parts of Europe, were to me just vague names. I met my grandparents on her side twice, maybe three times? I met most of my maternal cousins on a trip over there when I was nineteen, but I know I must have missed some, and the fact that I can't even name all of them lets you know how close we were. My father's side of the family was a similar story, only much closer geographically.

They all lived relatively close to the camp, about two hours from us. I had more interaction with them, but we still weren't having family reunions or anything. The closest we got was when we'd gather at my grandmother's house for Thanksgiving, and even then it was only whatever handful of people happened to be around at the time. I always thought it weird as a kid when friends of mine lived in the same city, often on the same street, as their grandparents or other relatives. That's just not how things were done.

I imagine things feel similar for my kids. My oldest sister and her six children live near Columbus, Ohio. The next sister lives in Florida. My younger sister and her three kids are all the way up in Maine. It's a pretty wide-spread, and one that makes it tough for my children to get to know their cousins. It also made it so that the whole family – parents, siblings, spouses, and kids – twenty-one people in all – had never all been in the same place at the same time. My father had always talked about wanting to have a great big tree set up in the front window of the cabin and have everybody together for Christmas sometime. Many months in advance, in the spring of 2019, my sisters and I started planning just such a trip. There was initially some doubt about whether everyone would be able to make it, and if we all could, could we make it a surprise?

It turns out that trying to surprise your father with a big tree and a weekend at the cabin with far fewer beds than attendees can be rather difficult. We were trying to keep the arrival of at least two of the siblings a secret, which required enlisting the help of my mother. What followed was a comedy of errors of bad sitcom level proportions, with various people trying to keep various secrets and failing in spectacular fashion.

I was able to borrow a fifteen-foot artificial tree from a friend, and, digging through our basement, came up with ten or so boxes of abandoned Christmas lights that had been spontaneously tying themselves in knots and then fossilizing for the last ten years. I arrived far enough in advance of everyone else that I was able to get everything set up and welcome the whole family with a fully decorated tree, artfully hung icicle lights on the front porch, and fresh baked Christmas cookies.

Uh-huh, sure.

The tree had about five different sections that would maybe fit together if you had an engineering degree. The self-stick hangers for the lights (Easy to apply! Great for outdoors!) stuck only to my gloves or to one another. The lights that had been abandoned in the basement turned out to have been abandoned for a reason – most of them didn't work at all, some would blink intermittently, and one strand would shoot pretty Christmas sparks from empty bulb sockets. I didn't even want to attempt the cookie thing.

The others began arriving long before anything had reached an even remotely festive appearance. My parents were the first ones to show up, along with my sister from Florida who had flown in and was staying with them. Apparently my own mother doesn't trust me enough to plan a Christmas feast, because even despite my assurances that I had taken care of the food, she brought along so much bread, pasta, and stuffing that a pack mule would not have gone unappreciated. My wife showed up with our kids a little later, then a nephew made his way in, followed closely by his parents and the rest of their kids. And now the extent of my family's trust in me was made clear when they each arrived with a stockpile of groceries, "Just in case." The only ones missing now were my youngest sister and her family. The newest addition for them was a little boy they had adopted only a few months prior. None of us had had the chance to meet him yet, so this would be a first introduction all the way around.

Their arrival was the one secret we managed to keep from both of my parents. The house was already quite packed by the time they showed up later that evening, and in the chaos the sudden appearance of a few more bodies didn't immediately register with either of my parents. I watched them from across the room as the realization finally hit them both that, for the first time, all their kids and grandkids were together. I wish I could say more about what transpired in that moment, but my eyes began to water uncontrollably for no apparent reason whatsoever. I think they probably unloaded more groceries.

The evening flew by, propelled by food, alcohol, card games, and political arguments. I don't know if there was really as much shouting as I remember, probably everyone was just trying to be heard over everyone else. The younger children dropped off to sleep periodically in whatever corner or on whatever available surface they could find. One nephew slept on the floor next to the water heater in the utility closet. My back was sore the next morning just thinking about it.

Christmas day saw more feasting and drinking and plenty of snowmen and kamikaze toboggan riding and board games. The kids all got to "Ooh and Ahh" over their newest cousin. Lots of photos were taken, lots of laughing, probably some more arguing. Someone hooked a line of sleds up to an ATV in an attempt to win multiple Darwin awards. It was pretty much what I had pictured in my head six months prior when we first began planning it.

I did a good bit of sitting on the porch just to get out of the house and all the commotion. At one point my father joined me outside. He's not really the emotional type, unless it's emotions like rage and fury when faced with someone driving slower than him. Or someone driving faster than him. Or someone driving the same speed but in the next lane over. But you could tell that he was happy. The two of us sat quietly on the porch for a bit. Outside, the sound of melting snow dripping from the cabin's metal roof, inside, the sound of what was probably a once in a lifetime family gathering.

"I don't know how you pulled it off, but this was something."

"Yeah, it was."

# Acknowledgments

I don't want this to sound like an awards show or anything, but I would like to thank a number of people who made this book possible, either by working on it directly or by being there during any of my outdoor experiences, whether included in these pages or not.

Thanks to MaryBeth, Jarrod, and Ken for their input and feedback as first readers, and especially for their encouragement.

For getting me involved in the outdoor life I'd like to thank the folks from LTA, especially Nat, Jim, Timmy, and Woz; my father for all those times he let me tag along; Fisher and Carla for getting me out west; Jamie for the Christmas tree and the broadheads; and all the hillbilly weekend camp crew, without whom much of the stupidity in this book would not have happened.

Special thanks to my family, all of them, who appear in these stories. Even if they would prefer that they had not.

www.ingramcontent.com/pod-product-compliance
Lightning Source LLC
Chambersburg PA
CBHW021341290326
41933CB00037B/317